GENESIS THREE WORLD

Mark T. Goodman, DMin.

GENESIS THREE WORLD

NAVIGATING THROUGH BROKENNESS

MARK T. GOODMAN, DMIN

GENESIS THREE WORLD: Navigating through Brokenness
by Mark T. Goodman, DMin.
Copyright © 2023 by Mark T. Goodman
All Rights Reserved.
ISBN: 978-1-59755-742-9

Published by: ADVANTAGE BOOKS™ Longwood, FL.
                 www.advbookstore.com

Library of Congress Catalog Number: 2023942381	
Name:	Goodman, Mark T., Author
Title:	*GENESIS THREE WORLD: Navigating through Brokenness*
	Mark T Goodman
	Advantage Books, 2023
Identifiers:	ISBN Paperback: 978159757429
Subjects:	

First Printing: September 2023
23 24 25 26 27 28   10 9 8 7 6 5 4 3 2 1

ENDORSEMENTS

Dr. Goodman takes a wholistic look from three different perspectives on what it is like to live in a Genesis Three World. The first perspective focuses on what we have lost through man's rebellion and the negative impact of sin entering God's perfect world. The second perspective describes the John Three response of a loving God in bringing redemption to His creation. The epistle of James provides the framework for regeneration of mankind through the sacrifice of God's Only Son. Finally, the author paints a picture through the promises of Revelation of what it looks like to live in Eden restored! The invitation is clear for all humanity: "Taste and see that the LORD is good."

- Dr. Randy Covington, Executive Director, Alaska Baptist Resource Network

As the lead pastor of a large congregation, I'm regularly approached with the same burning question. "If God is in control of the world, why did this terrible thing happen in my life." I've never really had a good answer until now. In this book, Mark wonderfully explains how the lingering effects of sin still have influence in our current culture. While as followers of Jesus, sin has no power over us, it still however looms in the everyday issues of life on planet earth. I found encouragement and strength on each page to fight the good fight, as I wait for the One who will come to set everything back in it's rightful order. As Mark points out, "In a broken world, our only hope is in Jesus." If you're struggling to understand how a follower of Jesus can live in victory in a fallen world, this book is for you. I highly recommend it.

– Larry Dugger, Lead Pastor at Family Church, Bestselling author

The Bible has always told us that this world is not our home. But we forget, and we wonder why things are so messy. Well, It is true, we live in a Genesis Three world. This book is beautifully crafted to give the reader an overarching image of how we live in this world by keeping our gaze fixed on Jesus. The book provides a road map through the whole bible, walking us through scripture, to better understand the darkness so that we can choose and seek, and run after living in the Light. This book reflects the beautiful story of faithfulness of the LORD in a renewed sense as Christians wait in the brokenness of this world but trusting and knowing Jesus is worth the wait! Jesus is the answer and this book gives us a deeper perspective through Scripture on how we faithfully wait because we know and trust Jesus is the solution. We wait in the knowing where we live today so that we anticipate our true home is not here and this book provides a Grand Canyon perspective on reality. This book gives the reader a Hope of which has always existed but with freshness to see clearly how we can navigate ourselves to be awake and alert for God in our every-day living for Him.

- Cherie Cobb, Pastor, White River Methodist Church

Dedication

For Vonda Kay . . .

*I agree with the words of God – it is not good for man to be alone.
I am not. Thank you for walking with me in this world. I love you!*

Table of Contents

Mark T. Goodman, DMin.

Introduction

Jesus is always the answer. Or so I thought. Around the time I earned my driver's license, I sat in Youth Group listening to our teacher. He asked the group the following question, "Who is the prince of this world?" As one raised in church since the womb (Thank you, Mom and Dad!), I, with confidence, quickly replied, "Jesus." I figured that our teacher would nod in approval and carry on. However, he responded with the verbal equivalent of a Red X. Then he read John 12:31.

John 12:31 – Now is the time for judgment on this world; now the prince of this world will be driven out.

Somehow, in my sixteen years and nine months of attending church, I had missed that verse, or at least failed to recall it.

Satan, the prince of our world?! How could that be? The answer is found in Genesis 3.

As a preacher / teacher, I am a John 3:16, Romans 12:1, Jude 21 guy. While I strive to declare *the whole counsel of God,* all my preaching and teaching are colored by those three verses. All my preaching and teaching are also written and proclaimed in light of Genesis 3. As I say regularly, we live in a Genesis Three World.

Sibs Sabanda, Executive Director of Faith and Work Alliance, writes,

Here is an interesting fact. There are only four chapters in the Bible without the distorting effects of sin – the first two and the last two. In the first two (Genesis 1 and 2), sin has not entered the world. In the last two (Revelation 21 and 22), John sees a vision of creation restored, where every stain of sin has been removed. Everything in between is the unfolding drama of human civilization in a world distorted by sin! Is it any wonder that we do not naturally seek out design? Is it any wonder that we so quickly dismiss certain aspects of Creation as being inherently secular? Is it any wonder at all! Because distortion so dominates the human story, the design chapter is almost completely overshadowed. The dirt and muck of sin's distortion all but covers up God's fingerprints in Creation to the point where we sometimes forget they are there! (48)

As the author of this book, my goals are as follows:

1. To explain my conviction that you and I live in a Genesis Three World.

2. To provide examples of the effects of Genesis 3 on our world.

3. To assist you in navigating your way in this Genesis Three World.

4. To show how the fact that we live in such a world is not the end of the world.

As the reader of this book, you will:

1. Be the judge of my success or failure in reaching my goals.

2. Be exposed to new ideas based on old truths.

Thank you for your interest. Thank you for taking the time to read my book. I trust that it will be time invested, not time wasted.

Now it's time to turn the page.

GENESIS THREE WORLD

A Definition

Noun: a world damaged by the sin of Adam and Eve, as depicted in the third chapter of Genesis, the first book in the Bible.

1

"THE STORY
OF
GENESIS THREE"

Long before John Steinbeck titled his most ambitious novel *East of Eden*, the writer of Genesis described Abel's murderous brother's place of residence.

> *Genesis 4:16 – So Cain went out from the Lord's presence and lived in the land of Nod, east of Eden.*

The description of Cain's location accomplishes more than placing a dot on a map. It identifies a condition. Upon creating Cain's parents, God placed them in Eden, a garden bearing the Hebrew name meaning "place of pleasure." Cain did not, nor did Adam and Eve for that matter, live in a place of pleasure. What went wrong?

Genesis chapter three tells the story.

To appreciate the magnitude of the third chapter of Genesis, one must understand the world as God made it and Adam and Eve experienced it. The first chapter of Genesis contains a simple yet deeply meaningful description of God's handiwork. Beginning with *"God saw that the light was good"* the chapter contains six God-saw-good moments. Then, when all His initial creative work was done …

> *Genesis 1:31a – God saw all that he had made, and it was very good.*

Genesis chapter two agrees with the goodness of all that God made. (The only not-good mention regards Adam's pre-Eve condition.) The chapter ends with a happy Adam and Eve living without shame. Oh, that that condition remained!! But sadly, conditions change drastically.

The shift began with a seemingly innocent question.

> *Genesis 3:1 – Now the serpent was more crafty than any of the wild animals the Lord God had made. He said to the woman, "Did God really say, 'You must not eat from any tree in the garden'?"*

The serpent (the one we discover later in Scripture who is the great deceiver) spawns doubt. In her reply to the serpent's question about the command of God, Eve responded …

> *Genesis 3:2-3 – "We may eat fruit from the trees in the garden, but God did say, 'You must not eat fruit from the tree that is in the middle of the garden, and you must not touch it, or you will die.'"*

She spoke words of direction more limiting than God actually provided. She correctly stated God's prohibition of eating from the tree of the knowledge of good and evil. She added a word about restriction of even touching the tree. Did Adam – just to be safe – add that when he passed on the direction he received from God? Did Eve overstate out of caution? We do not know. Ultimately – whatever the case – Eve, joined by Adam not long thereafter, touched and ate from the tree's fruit not intended for their consumption. Recall the "no shame" of Genesis chapter two? That condition was now no longer.

> *Genesis 3:7 – Then the eyes of both of them were opened, and they realized they were naked; so they sewed fig leaves together and made coverings for themselves.*

Doubting God led to disobeying God; disobeying God led to shame and fear.

> *Genesis 3:10 – He answered, "I heard you in the garden, and I was afraid because I was naked; so I hid."*

Shame and fear were quickly followed by more negative effects. Some of those effects are detailed in the third chapter of Genesis and others reveal their ugliness in the later stories of Scripture and the sad realities of today. Those effects will be the subject of the next seven chapters of this book.

Before we head into those chapters, the end of Genesis chapter three necessitates attention. As stated when we began, Cain lived east of Eden. In fact, Cain never saw Eden. Why? Because his parents left Eden (not a choice of their own) before his birth.

> *Genesis 3:23-24 – So the LORD God banished him from the Garden of Eden to work the ground from which he had been taken. After he drove the man out, he placed on the east side of the Garden of Eden cherubim and a flaming sword flashing back and forth to guard the way to the tree of life.*

The "him" undoubtedly includes a "her." Adam and Eve are shown the proverbial door. God placed them on the east side of the Garden of Eden and blocked their way (with flaming sword-wielding cherubim, no less) to prevent their reentry.

Before we move to seven chapters that will not be particularly encouraging, two observations from the closing verses of Genesis chapter three are important to make as they assure the reader that not all hope was lost.

First, God clothed the naked-and-ashamed couple.

> *Genesis 3:21 – The LORD God made garments of skin for Adam and his wife and clothed them.*

God knew that the fig-leaf skirt and loincloth (see 3:7) would not do the trick. So, at the cost of an animal's life (foreshadowing!), God clothed them.

Second, God protected them from eternally remaining in their state of not-walking-in-the-garden shame.

> *Genesis 3:22 – And the LORD God said, "The man has now become like one of us, knowing good and evil. He must not be*

allowed to reach out his hand and take also from the tree of life and eat, and live forever."

God loved them too much to leave them in the negative state into which they placed themselves. Animal-skin covered, and reentry disallowed, the couple walked out into a Genesis Three World. The world into which you and I were born.

2

"EVIDENCE OF BROKENNESS"

Cain grew angry and killed his brother. The pre-flood people's wickedness was great. Ham shamed his father. The post-flood people constructed a tower to their own glory. Sarai laughed at God. Lot's daughters conspired to bear children through incest. Peoples enslaved peoples. Moses killed a man. Moses hit a rock in anger. Aaron caved to pressure and built the infamous calf. Millions of Hebrew people rebelled. Events in Judges make readers cringe. Priests stole. Saul grew prideful. David caved to his lust.

Israel fell. Judah fell. At Herod's decree, Bethlehem's boys died. Nine lepers refused to say thank you. A house of prayer became a den of thieves. James and John selfishly requested front-row seats. Peter turned coward. Judas sold his soul. Jealous religious leaders saw to it that brutal Rome nailed Jesus to a cross.

James and Stephen died as martyrs. Ananias and Sapphira lied and dropped dead. Paul distrusted Mark. Brothers fought for power. Fellow church members disparaged one another. Corinthian people stuffed their faces rather than humbly share the Lord's Supper. Philemon wanted his slave returned. John lived on a deserted island. Genocides made way for expanding kingdoms.

Religious bodies kill in the name of proper religion. People enslave people. World and Civil Wars tear apart families. Towers fall. Women are abused. Children are neglected. Students shoot students. Needles enter arms. Desperate men swallow pills. Lies are told. Banks fail. Disease spreads. People traffic people. Races divide. Dreams are crushed. Societies pervert sex. Greed takes lives.

Shame. Fear. Sadness. Starvation. Murder. Selfishness. Hopelessness. Pride.

Things are not as they should be. Headmaster Thomas Arnold spoke words of reality into his students and rugby players – "[life] was no fool's or sluggard's paradise into which he had wandered by chance, but a battlefield ordained from of old, where there are no spectators but the youngest must take his side, and the stakes are life and death" (qtd in Bowie 509).

In the words of Paul, *"the creation was subjected to frustration"* (Romans 8:20).

3

"EFFECTS ON FAMILY"

God saw that it was not good for Adam to be alone. In Genesis, chapter three, Adam disagreed. God confronted the fig-leaf-loincloth-wearing Adam about his disobedience. In reply the man said …

> *Genesis 3:12* – *"The woman you put here with me—she gave me some fruit from the tree, and I ate it."*

His "Wow!" upon seeing God's gift of Eve turned to "Woe, is me." Once thankful of his new companion, he now blames her for his own failure. The blaming did not stop there. *"The woman you put here"* Adam says. Up until that point all that Adam confessed was that he knew he was naked. The blaming of God and Eve marked Adam's first line of defense.

Even though that line of defense fails, the use of it continues to this day. Individuals sin and whole families suffer.

Marriage

With the possible exception of divorce attorneys, most everyone agrees that the divorce rate remains far too high. For many couples "'til death do us part" has become "'til annoyance / unexpected stress / preconceived ideas do us part." Adam's *The woman you put here with me"* is echoed as husbands and wives blame each other without taking personal responsibility.

Did Eve give Adam the fruit? Yes. But Adam took it. Not only did he take it, but he was also with Eve when she took her bite.

From a biblical point of view, marriage is a covenant between one man and one woman based on commitment and mutual love. Sometimes marriages work without the second of these; they rarely make it without the first. Commitment is the glue that makes marriage work. Love is important, too. One must be clear on the definition of love. Romantic love draws couples together; love that is described so well by Paul holds couples together.

1 Corinthians 13:4-8a – Love is patient, love is kind. It does not envy, it does not boast, it is not proud. It does not dishonor others, it is not self-seeking, it is not easily angered, it keeps no record of wrongs. Love does not delight in evil but rejoices with the truth. It always protects, always trusts, always hopes, always perseveres. Love never fails.

Notice that last brief sentence. If love never fails, why do so many couples end their covenants of marriage? Because one person or both fail to love. Love never fails. People fail to love. In this Genesis Three World, we find …

- Husbands keep a record of wrongs.

- Wives lose patience.

- Couples fail to be kind.

- Once gentlemanly grooms carelessly grow in pride.

- Once radiant brides discover how to seek after self.

Things are not as they should be.

Siblings

Cain killed Abel. Cain's actions were not an accident or done in self-defense. Cain planned Abel's death. Cain committed premeditated murder.

Genesis 4:6-7 – Then the Lord said to Cain, "Why are you angry? Why is your face downcast? If you do what is right, will you not be accepted? But if you do not do what is right, sin is crouching at your door; it desires to have you, but you must rule over it."

God gave Cain time to cool off. Cain refused to take it.

Since the occasion of the one worthy and one faulty offering, brothers (and sisters) have compared their efforts. Thankfully, rarely does such comparison lead to death; nevertheless, comparison often leads to disunity. In this Genesis Three World, brothers boast and sisters pull hair. Siblings living in loving unity spread joy. Siblings living in self-focused rivalry leave damage as they go.

Parents and Children

As mentioned in the previous chapter, most of the events recorded in the Old Testament book of Judges prove to be not for the weak of heart. The misuse of humanity by other humans causes one's stomach to turn. And it's not just Judges. Stories of violence are not hard to find in the pages of Scripture. The particularly troubling accounts are those involving the suffering of children. The Bible mentions (briefly, thankfully) the practice of child sacrifice, an unconscionable practice. While that practice clearly and thankfully is a far extreme, one of the results of this broken world is divisiveness between parents and their children. Parents harm children. Children mock parents.

While the overly-driven dad does not place his son on an altar of sacrifice, he does sacrifice his relationship with him as he stays longer at the office, missing his son's solo in the school concert. While the image-focused mom does not raise a pagan priest's blade, she does cause tears to flow down her daughter's cheeks as she tells her that she needs to look just one certain way, a way made possible only by editing tools.

While today's children would never think of removing their father from a position of power to take over his spot . . . on second thought, do they?

We do not live in a day of sons knocking off dads to take the throne. But we do live in a day when children choose disrespect over honor. How many aging adults sit looking out the window hoping to see their child come by for a visit?

4

"EFFECTS ON SEX"

According to Genesis 3, one of the first results of the Fall, was human shame regarding their newly observed nakedness. Genesis 2 gave way to Genesis 3.

> *Genesis 2:25 – Adam and his wife were both naked, and they felt no shame.*

> *Genesis 3:7 – Then the eyes of both of them were opened, and they realized they were naked; so they sewed fig leaves together and made coverings for themselves.*

The next time the Bible mentions nakedness is that of drunk and disrobed Noah (of ark fame). With just a few page turns, the reader finds the lustful men of Sodom and the desperate act of Lot's daughters with their drunk father.

I have not counted; but if memory serves, the number of references in the Bible to sexual abuse and misuse far outnumber those of mutual pleasure and tenderness.

Unfortunately, that pattern holds. Perverted versions of sexuality abound. A few swipes of the thumb can bring images and videos to anyone old enough to operate a phone. Teenagers driven by God-given hormones receive no guidance as to how to handle them well. The numbers of cohabitation, with benefits, continue to grow as the bond between sex and marriage loosens by the day. While the outlook on properly handled sex is not hopeless, it is in a sad state of affairs.

And that raises the topic of affairs. The vast majority of people frown upon the practice of polygamy – official polygamy that is. Few indeed attempt to exchange vows with two or more spouses simultaneously; yet far too many (one case is too many) practice sexual polygamy.

None of this should be. However, in this Genesis Three World, the effects of sin on sex continue.

5

"EFFECTS ON THE CHURCH"

Not even the gates of hell will overcome the Church. Jesus promised as much. I am glad He did for several times throughout the past twenty centuries have been difficult for Jesus' Bride. Extreme cases such as corrupt teachers and pedophile preachers have bruised the Church. Less extreme and more prevalent cases occur within local bodies as church members argue over such items as carpet color, instrument choices, and personnel salaries. Similar damage is caused when church pastors and church elders and/or deacons engage in tug-of-war like grabs for power or simply do not get along.

All one needs to do to understand that things have been broken within the Church from nearly day one is read the Apostle Paul's two letters to the Christians in Corinth as found in the New Testament. We begin to grasp their much-like-today faults when we read passages such as these...

1 Corinthians 3:1-4 – Brothers and sisters, I could not address you as people who live by the Spirit but as people who are still worldly—mere infants in Christ. I gave you milk, not solid food, for you were not yet ready for it. Indeed, you are still not ready. You are still worldly. For since there is jealousy and quarreling among you, are you not worldly? Are you not acting like mere humans? For when one says, "I follow Paul," and another, "I follow Apollos," are you not mere human beings?

1 Corinthians 4:18-21 – Some of you have become arrogant, as if I were not coming to you. But I will come to you very soon, if the Lord is willing, and then I will find out not only how these arrogant people are talking, but what power they have. For the kingdom of

God is not a matter of talk but of power. What do you prefer? Shall I come to you with a rod of discipline, or shall I come in love and with a gentle spirit?

And . . .

1 Corinthians 11:17-18 – In the following directives I have no praise for you, for your meetings do more harm than good. In the first place, I hear that when you come together as a church, there are divisions among you, and to some extent I believe it.

Anglicans, Baptists, Catholics, Methodists, and Presbyterians alike come in as many varieties as the combined flavors of Baskin-Robbins and Ben & Jerry's. While much good fruit has grown out of the continued growth-by-split occurrences, so has much hurt. Ministers quit. Members flee. Children actually do depart from the way they should go. As a Christian and a pastor, I love the Bride of Christ. I have the privilege of serving and leading a church in Anchorage, Alaska. Our church is loving, healthy, and active in serving. By the grace of God, we are united and working together. All that established, I have known the pains of ministry both here and in other places of service. One place even took a toll on my health. I wish that was an anomaly. Unfortunately, it is common.

6

"EFFECTS ON TIME"

Some say it is a special construct. Others refer to it as an illusion. Einstein called it relative (as you have experienced if you've been in a car accident when seconds feel like minutes). Whatever it is, time is a key element of life and as Steve Miller warns us, it keeps on "slippin' into the future."

Like each of the areas we have covered so far, time is negatively affected by the sin in this Genesis Three World. For example, some people drift toward the wasting of time. They remain idle as time slips. Sin kills the motivations to honor God with time and, therefore, leads to two extremes in time wasting. Slothfulness and Busybodiedness. As one sits passive, the other spins their wheels and not much of any value moves into the "Accomplished" folder.

Another result of sin on time is infatuation with the past. We do well to learn from and enjoy memories from the past. I am thankful for the decades-old home videos my dad made of interviews of a now-deceased generation of Goodmans. I enjoy viewing old photos and pulling out the dust-covered slides (remember slides?). You have similar past-oriented traditions as well. Those are good. Remember even Jesus points us to the past each time we take the Bread and Wine in *remembrance of me*. None of those secular or religious activities call for a dwelling in the past; they offer memories, not tents.

> *Luke 9:33 — As the men were leaving Jesus, Peter said to him, "Master, it is good for us to be here. Let us put up three shelters— one for you, one for Moses and one for Elijah." (He did not know what he was saying.)*

Peter, in trying to make sense of a beyond-comprehension occurrence, attempted to set up camp. The Father, as He always does, had a better plan. A perfect plan.

> *Luke 9:34-35 – While he was speaking, a cloud appeared and covered them, and they were afraid as they entered the cloud. A voice came from the cloud, saying, "This is my Son, whom I have chosen; listen to him."*

Part of listening to (and heeding) Jesus is living each "Today" with an eye on "Tomorrow." No matter how good your good ol' days were, they are no place for you today.

Yet another result of sin on time is obsession with the future. You may be asking, "Didn't you just write 'an eye on tomorrow,' Mark?" Yes, I did. However, "an eye on" and "obsession" are not the same thing. "An eye on" leads to achieved goals, fulfilled dreams, self-restraint, and secure retirement – to name a few benefits. Obsession leads to anxiety, selfishness, missing great "now" moments, helicopter and/or live-my-unmet-dreams-for-me parents – to name a few damages.

> *Ecclesiastes 3:1-8 – There is a time for everything,*
> *and a season for every activity under the heavens:*
> *a time to be born and a time to die,*
> *a time to plant and a time to uproot,*
> *a time to kill and a time to heal,*
> *a time to tear down and a time to build,*
> *a time to weep and a time to laugh,*
> *a time to mourn and a time to dance,*
> *a time to scatter stones and a time to gather them,*
> *a time to embrace and a time to refrain from embracing,*
> *a time to search and a time to give up,*
> *a time to keep and a time to throw away,*
> *a time to tear and a time to mend,*
> *a time to be silent and a time to speak,*
> *a time to love and a time to hate,*
> *a time for war and a time for peace.*

7

"EFFECTS ON VOCATION"

Back in the Genesis Two World, God gave Adam a gift, the gift of vocation.

Genesis 2:15 – The LORD God took the man and put him in the Garden of Eden to work it and take care of it.

Notice that the "work" and "take care" responsibilities arrived before sin, not as a result of sin. Vocation was God's idea and, therefore, a good idea. Much of vocation remains positive. However much of vocation is broken as well.

Think …

- Underpaid workers
- Sweat shops
- Abusive bosses
- Unethical employees
- Workplace discrimination

Think …

- Aches and pains
- Workplace injuries
- Sour customers
- Drought-ruined crops
- Pesty pests

Without the "ers," the sign still makes sense.

Fields fill with thorns. Boardrooms create burn-out. Workers grow weary. These problems occur because we live in a Genesis Three World.

What would it be like for the average worker to enjoy vocation as much as vacation? Adam knew the answer. Pre-Genesis Three, his work was a joy not a burden. Imagine his joy as he accomplished the tasks God assigned to him.

Genesis 2:19-20a – Now the LORD God had formed out of the ground all the wild animals and all the birds in the sky. He brought them to the man to see what he would name them; and whatever the man called each living creature, that was its name. So the man gave names to all the livestock, the birds in the sky and all the wild animals.

While God was the Creator, Adam was the inventor of names. He used his God-given wisdom and language to identify the creatures God formed. During his pre-shame days, Adam surely enjoyed the naming as well as the tending. His burden was light.

But then he and his bride questioned, doubted, and ignored God; and work became a heavy burden.

Genesis 3:17-19 – To Adam he said, "Because you listened to your wife and ate fruit from the tree about which I commanded you, 'You must not eat from it,' Cursed is the ground because of you; through painful toil you will eat food from it all the days of your life. It will produce thorns and thistles for you, and you will eat the plants of the field. By the sweat of your brow you will eat your food until you return to the ground, since from it you were taken; for dust you are and to dust you will return."

Today the struggles with work continue. Job dissatisfaction impacts millions. Job insecurity does the same. Verbal and physical assaults occur in offices and factories as employees reach their wits' ends.

The frustrated teacher of three millennia ago voiced his exasperation.

<u>Ecclesiastes 2:17-23</u> – So I hated life, because the work that is done under the sun was grievous to me. All of it is meaningless, a chasing after the wind. I hated all the things I had toiled for under the sun, because I must leave them to the one who comes after me. And who knows whether that person will be wise or foolish? Yet they will have control over all the fruit of my toil into which I have poured my effort and skill under the sun. This too is meaningless. So my heart began to despair over all my toilsome labor under the sun. For a person may labor with wisdom, knowledge and skill, and then they must leave all they own to another who has not toiled for it. This too is meaningless and a great misfortune. What do people get for all the toil and anxious striving with which they labor under the sun? All their days their work is grief and pain; even at night their minds do not rest. This too is meaningless.

8

"EFFECTS ON JOY"

In reference to Satan, Jesus warned his hearers …

John 10:10a – The thief comes only to steal and kill and destroy…

As a pastor, I meet with people to help them grow in their faith. Just as vines and trees grow best when their unhealthy branches are removed, we ever-growing humans flourish when we remove our wounds and brokenness through honest confession, repentance, forgiveness, and a good ol' dose of lettin' it go.

Unfortunately, we tend to hold tightly to the pain of our pasts and give frustrations and letdowns more attention than successes and victories. Whether the results are more the work of Satan or simply our lack of faith, they add up to the same thing – the loss of Joy.

Several years ago, my oldest son played on a YMCA basketball team. I enjoyed watching him and his dribbling friends enjoy the games. They did well. In fact, they won every game except one. One. After their last game, their coach gathered them around him and handed them their well-earned trophies. Then he said it. "Guys, good job! We did well this season. We could have done better, but we did well."

"We could have done better."

True? Yes.

Needed saying? No!

Those boys lost one game. But, more importantly, those boys won all the rest. And, even more importantly, they learned new skills, got exercise, learned sportsmanship, and had fun.

I am not calling my son's coach "Satan." In fact, he is a good guy who I often see and exchange "hellos" with at the gym. Yet, the illustration is clear. Jesus highlights our wins and covers our losses with His blood.

Satan highlights our losses and covers our wins with guilt. As for me, I'm choosing Jesus.

God told Jeremiah …

Jeremiah 31:34b – *"For I will forgive their wickedness and will remember their sins no more."*

Paul encouraged the Corinthians …

2 Corinthians 5:18-19a – *All this is from God, who reconciled us to himself through Christ and gave us the ministry of reconciliation: that God was reconciling the world to himself in Christ, not counting people's sins against them.*

Yet – even still – for so many people, the regrets of yesterday cling. Their joy is buried under a pile of old laundry. And while clean clothes are folded and ready, they heed the father of lies and rewear the stinky socks and stained shirt. They dress in the Genesis Three World uniform.

How sad would it have been if King David chose to stay in the slimy pit full of mud and mire? (See Psalm 40.)

What if we remembered Rahab as merely a prostitute and not a hero in Jericho? (See Joshua 2.)

Imagine if when self-aware Simon Peter said, "Go away from me, Lord; I am a sinful man!" Jesus agreed and walked away? (See Luke 5:8.)

What if when the same Simon, post-denial, went back to fishing, never dropped his nets, and swam back to shore? (See John 21.)

9

"SEVEN DEADLY SIN-STAINS"

Evagrius Ponticus, one of the Desert Fathers of the fourth century AD, wrote and warned about nine sins. Over time those nine sins were recategorized into what Pope Gregory I deemed the seven deadly sins (seven categories into which all sins fall). The original sin of Eden's couple opened the door to the sins and the occurrence of sins that outnumber the population of the globe. The categories are as follows: Lust, Gluttony, Greed, Sloth, Wrath, Envy, Pride.

Their opposites are:

- Chastity

- Temperance

- Charity

- Diligence

- Patience

- Gratitude

- Humility

In today's world, both the sins and the virtues remain. The sins are the stains in the Genesis Three World.

Lust

The men of Sodom lusted after Lot's guests. Lot's daughters committed incest with their father. Judah hired a prostitute who, unbeknownst to him, was his daughter-in-law. Potiphar's wife lusted for Joseph. Those examples are all found in just the first book of the Bible. Lust spreads throughout the next sixty-five.

Gluttony

Judges 3:21-22 – Ehud reached with his left hand, drew the sword from his right thigh and plunged it into the king's belly. Even the handle sank in after the blade, and his bowels discharged. Ehud did not pull the sword out, and the fat closed in over it.

1 Samuel 4:18 - When he mentioned the ark of God, Eli fell backward off his chair by the side of the gate. His neck was broken and he died, for he was an old man, and he was heavy. He had led Israel forty years.

Those are extreme examples, perhaps; yet kings and priests are not the only people who struggle with gluttony. Gluttony leads people astray as they indulge in food, overwork, glue themselves to TV, obsess over athletes, allow sex to rule over them, and any number of practices through which they take good things to extremes.

"Just one more plate." "Only one more drink." "I can stop any time I want." "I'll sleep when I'm dead." "YOLO." The cries of the glutton ring out in this Genesis Three World.

Greed

Magicians pull rabbits out of hats and doves out of white handkerchiefs. God makes quail come out of Israelite noses.

Numbers 11:18-20 – "Tell the people: 'Consecrate yourselves in preparation for tomorrow, when you will eat meat. The LORD heard you when you wailed, "If only we had meat to eat! We were better off in Egypt!" Now the LORD will give you meat, and you will eat it. You will not eat it for just one day, or two days, or five, ten or twenty days, but for a whole month—until it comes out of your nostrils and you loathe it—because you have rejected the LORD, who is among you, and have wailed before him, saying, "Why did we ever leave Egypt?"'"

Hyperbole, for sure. Yet a vivid picture, nonetheless. The greed of the meat-loving wanderers proved to backfire. Greed robs the disadvantaged. Greed leads to unethical practices. Greed stomps out the "little guy." Greed even costs lives.

<u>Sloth</u>

To clarify, we're referring to the action (inaction, more appropriately), not the barely-mobile-tree-gripping animal. Sloths (the furry type) are the only ones allowed to be slothful. Nevertheless two-legged creatures rest their way into this sin. To caution against such a willful habit, Paul reminded the Christians in Thessalonica of his rule …

> *2 Thessalonians 3:10* – *"The one who is unwilling to work shall not eat."*

Likewise, widows who were not busy but rather busybodies were not allowed in the lines for food-distributing deacons. Paul's rules were not targeting the poor. They were warning the willfully lazy.

> *[The fourth-century Desert Christians'] favored name for the vice comes from the Greek compound "a-kedia," which means "a lack of care." This does not mean simple: carelessness," but an intentional stance of "I could care less" – as in "I am not invested in this, so do not expect me to make an effort. Just let me stay where I am comfortable, would you?" The person with the vice of sloth, or acedia, is not passively suffering depression or torpor, but is actively refusing to care, to be moved. (DeYoung, 12)*

<u>Wrath</u>

Just as Isaiah prophesied, Jesus' arrived as the Prince of Peace. He blessed peacemakers and taught turning of cheeks. Paul, once driven by religiously-funded wrath, taught peace to Christians in Rome.

> *Romans 12:19* – *Do not take revenge, my dear friends, but leave room for God's wrath, for it is written: "It is mine to avenge; I will repay," says the Lord.*

Read once more the warning God gave to Cain.

Genesis 4:6-7 – Then the LORD said to Cain, "Why are you angry? Why is your face downcast? If you do what is right, will you not be accepted? But if you do not do what is right, sin is crouching at your door; it desires to have you, but you must rule over it."

Anger arises in all people. In this Genesis Three World, anger often grows into wrath.

Envy

He's an easy target so I'll mention Cain again. He envied God's response to Abel at the giving of sacrifices. God knew the danger of envy and, therefore, He included it, by a different name, in the Ten Commandments.

Deuteronomy 5:21 – "You shall not covet your neighbor's wife. You shall not set your desire on your neighbor's house or land, his male or female servant, his ox or donkey, or anything that belongs to your neighbor."

Think of the damage caused by envy / covetousness. Friendships are lost. Lives are taken. Contentment is robbed.

Pride

Here I use a different word associated with this particular category of sin. I do so because pride can be positive. Healthy pride is appropriate satisfaction in a job / effort well done. So, let's go with vainglory. Vainglory expresses itself through boasting. Vainglory struts and brags. It's the touchdown dance gone too far. It's the comparison of GPAs with boastfulness in your score.

Paul Cadmus, the mid-twentieth century artist, painted a vividly disturbing series of pieces – seven – one for each of The Seven Deadly Sins. Of them he said, "I don't appear as myself, but I am all of the Deadly Sins in a way, as you all are, too." His truth hits home. Well said, Paul. Well said.

10

"FINDING COMFORT
IN DISCOMFORT"

The conversation in my Men's Life Group continued, but I was disconnected. I wasn't daydreaming; I was pondering. Moments before Kevin (not his real name) shared how, in his darkest days of alcohol and drug addiction, he found "comfort in discomfort." He continued by saying, "Whatever [substance] I could get in my body to numb the pain." Using discomfort to numb the pain. That habit did not originate with Kevin. It is as old as the hills. It is also as current as today. The numbers, while not all-telling, indicate a problem.

Almost 21 million Americans have at least 1 addiction, yet only 10% of them receive treatment.

Drug overdose deaths have more than tripled since 1990.

Alcohol and drug addiction cost the U.S. economy over $600 billion every year.

About 20% of Americans who have depression, or an anxiety disorder also have a substance use disorder.

Source: AddictionCenter.com

And those numbers include only addictions to drugs and alcohol. Addiction comes in near endless varieties: sex, power, distraction, social media, cellphone games, work, recreation, hoarding. We are comfort seekers.

The freed Hebrew slaves longed to return to the discomfort of enslavement rather than face the unknowns of the wilderness. All the

Hebrew spies, except Caleb and Joshua, voted to stay in those same unknowns in order to avoid a new adventure in a promised land. Solomon's addiction to sex overrode his wisdom and killed his kingdom. King Xerxes' love of drink led him to pronounce a death sentence on the Jews. The discomforts of life continue to provide comfort.

John withholds his name but shares his story.

> *John 5:1-6 – Some time later, Jesus went up to Jerusalem for one of the Jewish festivals. Now there is in Jerusalem near the Sheep Gate a pool, which in Aramaic is called Bethesda and which is surrounded by five covered colonnades. Here a great number of disabled people used to lie—the blind, the lame, the paralyzed. One who was there had been an invalid for thirty-eight years. When Jesus saw him lying there and learned that he had been in this condition for a long time, he asked him, "Do you want to get well?"*

What a strange question for Jesus to ask! But was it? The biblical text informs us that the man *"had been an invalid for thirty-eight years."* The man was limited in mobility for nearly four decades. Why would Jesus ask him if he wanted to be healed? Perhaps the man found comfort in discomfort. As an invalid, he received food from good-hearted passersby and perhaps family members. Healing would mean taking up his mat and walking into a life of responsibility – finding a job, showing up to work, creating new habits, etc.

Physical disability is not required in choosing to stay. In this Genesis Three World, far too often people choose to continue in a life of discomfort, ignoring Jesus' invitation to take His burden that is light rather than the burdens of this world. Flowing from the gospel are freedom, security, rescue, redemption, restoration, cleansing, forgiveness, and salvation. Yet some (more often than not) choose to continue to live in their discomfort.

> *Matthew 19:16-22 – Just then a man came up to Jesus and asked, "Teacher, what good thing must I do to get eternal life?" "Why do you ask me about what is good?" Jesus replied. "There is only One who is good. If you want to enter life, keep the*

commandments." "Which ones?" he inquired. Jesus replied, "'You shall not murder, you shall not commit adultery, you shall not steal, you shall not give false testimony, honor your father and mother,' and 'love your neighbor as yourself.'" "All these I have kept," the young man said. "What do I still lack?" Jesus answered, "If you want to be perfect, go, sell your possessions and give to the poor, and you will have treasure in heaven. Then come, follow me." When the young man heard this, he went away sad, because he had great wealth.

If we could have asked his neighbors, their common answer would certainly have been that the man was happy. He was, after all, rich. Ask him, however, and you would have received a different answer. He discovered that his wealth was not enough; he longed for something more, for assurance that he would obtain eternal life. By all accounts, especially his own, he was a good man. He kept the Law of Moses and lived a life of peace. He practiced religion and regularly attended worship services. He fit the bill. The man expected Jesus to provide assurance that he was on the right track – the track to eternal life. Yet Jesus responded differently than the wealthy man expected.

Matthew 19:21 – *"If you want to be perfect, go, sell your possessions and give to the poor, and you will have treasure in heaven. Then come, follow me."*

And …

Matthew 19:22 – *When the young man heard this, he went away sad, because he had great wealth.*

Why did the man leave in rejection? Because although his soul was restlessly seeking assurance, he was unwilling to surrender his prized possessions. He found comfort in his wealth and chose to live in the discomfort of wondering if his eternal future was secure.

11

"IT'S BROKE; HE'LL FIX IT"

Walter Bowie wrote "The religion of the O.T. has in it always a virile optimism. It is not blind to the tragedy of life, but all the while it looks forward to triumph. Men and nations in their struggles against temptation and in their warfare against evil are meant not to surrender but to prevail" (509).

Like people of Jewish faith, Christians are thankful for the Hebrew Scriptures (the Old Testament). The first testament tells the backstory. It assures the reader that earthly existence is a carefully and orderly designed work of the Almighty Creator. The testament provides guidance, counsel, direction, needed conviction, and hope for an abundant future. Yet, from a Christian perspective, the Hebrew Scriptures are incomplete. Not that they need to be edited or added to but that they leave the reader wanting. For that reason, Christians, with even more gratitude, thank God for the second testament, the New Testament.

In rabbinic tradition, the readers of the holy text alter, verbally, the reading of the conclusion of the prophetic words of Malachi. The text reads …

Malachi 4:5-6 – "See, I will send the prophet Elijah to you before that great and dreadful day of the LORD comes. He will turn the hearts of the parents to their children, and the hearts of the children to their parents; or else I will come and strike the land with total destruction."

In verbal tradition, the rabbi reads the text as such …

Malachi 4:5-6, 5 – "See, I will send the prophet Elijah to you before that great and dreadful day of the LORD comes. He will turn the hearts of the parents to their children, and the hearts of the children to their parents; or else I will come and strike the land with total destruction. See, I will send the prophet Elijah to you before that great and dreadful day of the LORD comes."

Rather than leave his people hearing Scripture end with a promise of *"total destruction,"* he repeats the promise of verse five – that God would send the prophet Elijah. He would send a hero of old. A prophet of fame. An encourager of Israel. A light shining in the darkness.

Picking up where the Old Testament promise left off, Mark, the writer of the first (historically) gospel record, wrote …

Mark 1:1-8 – The beginning of the good news about Jesus the Messiah, the Son of God, as it is written in Isaiah the prophet: "I will send my messenger ahead of you, who will prepare your way"— "a voice of one calling in the wilderness, 'Prepare the way for the Lord, make straight paths for him.'"

And so, John the Baptist appeared in the wilderness, preaching a baptism of repentance for the forgiveness of sins. The whole Judean countryside and all the people of Jerusalem went out to him. Confessing their sins, they were baptized by him in the Jordan River. John wore clothing made of camel's hair, with a leather belt around his waist, and he ate locusts and wild honey. And this was his message: "After me comes the one more powerful than I, the straps of whose sandals I am not worthy to stoop down and untie. I baptize you with water, but he will baptize you with the Holy Spirit."

John, the New Testament's Elijah, did more than gather people by the river and baptize them; he directed their attention away from himself toward the *"one more powerful than I, the straps of whose sandals I am not worthy to stoop down and untie."* The more-powerful-One-than-John soon thereafter proclaimed …

Mark 1:15 – "The time has come," he said. "The kingdom of God has come near. Repent and believe the good news!"

Luke, another of the four gospel writers, recorded some of Jesus' earliest words …

Luke 4:18-19 – "The Spirit of the Lord is on me, because he has anointed me to proclaim good news to the poor.

He has sent me to proclaim freedom for the prisoners and recovery of sight for the blind, to set the oppressed free, to proclaim the year of the Lord's favor."

Jesus' arrival stood as evidence, for those with eyes to see, that while the world was broken, God was going to fix it. The Father promised to fix it right after Adam and Eve broke it. We find that promise in the very chapter that contains the story of the beginning of the brokenness within the words of God while speaking to the crafty serpent.

Genesis 3:14-15 – So the LORD God said to the serpent, "Because you have done this, "Cursed are you above all livestock and all wild animals! You will crawl on your belly and you will eat dust all the days of your life. And I will put enmity between you and the woman, and between your offspring and hers; he will crush your head, and you will strike his heel."

Biblical scholars refer to the promise contained in verse fifteen as the protoevangelium, a compound of two Greek words meaning "the first good news" (About-Jesus.org). Scholars also agree that the Old Testament contains hundreds more messianic promises – anywhere between 200 to 400.

One need not look only to the messianic promises to discover signs of the ultimate act of God restoring all things.

- God spared Cain.
- God saved Noah and his family from the Flood.

- God provided the rainbow, a visual reminder of the covenant.

- God chose Abram.

- God freed the enslaved Jews.

- God split the Sea.

- God provided pillars of cloud and fire.

- God provided water and manna.

- God provided the Law.

- God provided a new land.

- God won their battles.

- God sent prophets.

Clearly, God wanted His people to know that their actions, while costly, were not powerful enough to ruin beyond repair God's creative work. Stupidity does not supplant sovereignty. Sin does not own the last word.

12

"GENESIS 3 MEET JOHN 3"

After referring to our world as the Genesis Three World one Sunday, I received an inquiring email from a sincere-in-heart church member. Upon pondering my comment, she sent this question, "Do we live in a Genesis Three World, or do we live in an Acts One World?" This was my response to that email …

Thank you for reaching out with your question. When I refer to the world in which we live as the Genesis Three World, I am recognizing that sin continues to impact the world. Indeed, as Jesus said, Satan is the prince of the world (thankfully, however, not the King!). Jesus defeated him on the cross. As we wait for the second coming of Christ the Victor, we are secure in our salvation, but also still impacted by sin.

To answer your questions:

> *1. You are not seen as a sinner You are a daughter of God who (like all of us) continues to sin.*
>
> *2. We live in a world that is both "Genesis 3" and "Acts 1." The victory is won but the battles continue.*

When I say that we are in a Genesis Three World, it is also a reminder that we live not for this world but for the next.

We live in a Genesis Three World and an Acts One World. We also live in a John Three World. After providing the biblical record of Jesus' conversation with Nicodemus, the Pharisee with an open mind, John added explanation – explanation that contains what became the most well-known words of Scripture.

John 3:16-21 – For God so loved the world that he gave his one and only Son, that whoever believes in him shall not perish but have eternal life. For God did not send his Son into the world to condemn the world, but to save the world through him. Whoever believes in him is not condemned, but whoever does not believe stands condemned already because they have not believed in the name of God's one and only Son. This is the verdict: Light has come into the world, but people loved darkness instead of light because their deeds were evil. Everyone who does evil hates the light, and will not come into the light for fear that their deeds will be exposed. But whoever lives by the truth comes into the light, so that it may be seen plainly that what they have done has been done in the sight of God.

Genesis three meet John three

Genesis three, as we have established, states the problem. John three introduces the Answer.

I'm usually a soda and snacks-in-hand guy when I watch movies in theatres. I made an exception for Mel Gibson's *The Passion of the Christ.* Sweets and snacking did not seem appropriate for the occasion. While I still agree with my abstinence, I also know that the events portrayed in that movie move believers to taste and see that the Lord is good. The scribe of Hebrews chose rich wording when he wrote . . .

Hebrews 12:1-3 – Therefore, since we are surrounded by such a great cloud of witnesses, let us throw off everything that hinders and the sin that so easily entangles. And let us run with perseverance the race marked out for us, fixing our eyes on Jesus, the pioneer and perfecter of faith. For the joy set before him he endured the cross, scorning its shame, and sat down at the right hand of the throne of God. Consider him who endured such opposition from sinners, so that you will not grow weary and lose heart.

Notice the words about Jesus' emotion.

Hebrews 12:2b – For the joy set before him he endured the cross, scorning its shame, and sat down at the right hand of the throne of God.

"For the joy set before Him" ... Jesus did not take joy in suffering on the cross; He took joy in knowing what His suffering would bring about.

In Gibson's film is a scene that moves me each time I see it (and even as I think about it as I write this sentence). In the scene, actor Jim Caviezel, portraying Jesus, prays through tears to His Father for *"this cup to pass."* In that scene, Gibson uses poetic license, appropriately I believe, in placing Satan there in the garden. Surely Satan did not tempt Jesus only three years before and cease.

Luke 4:13 – When the devil had finished all this tempting, he left him until an opportune time.

As Satan, portrayed by Italian actress Rosalina Celentano, encroaches on Jesus, he releases a serpent. Jesus overcomes the temptation, arises, and crushes the head of the snake. (YouTube it. It's worth it!)

Genesis 3:15 – "And I will put enmity between you and the woman, and between your offspring and hers; he will crush your head, and you will strike his heel."

The scene is brilliant. The real-life crushing is more so. John, chapter three, explains how such a crushing was accomplished.

John 3:16-17 – For God so loved the world that he gave his one and only Son, that whoever believes in him shall not perish but have eternal life. For God did not send his Son into the world to condemn the world, but to save the world through him.

- God loved.
- God gave.

God loved and, therefore, gave His only Son so that all who would believe in Him will be spared the ultimate result of brokenness and receive wholeness. Paul, the apostle, rejoiced in this truth and urged others to join him in rejoicing.

Romans 8:28-39 – And we know that in all things God works for the good of those who love him, who have been called according to his purpose. For those God foreknew he also predestined to be conformed to the image of his Son, that he might be the firstborn among many brothers and sisters. And those he predestined, he also called; those he called, he also justified; those he justified, he also glorified.

What, then, shall we say in response to these things? If God is for us, who can be against us? He who did not spare his own Son, but gave him up for us all—how will he not also, along with him, graciously give us all things? Who will bring any charge against those whom God has chosen? It is God who justifies. Who then is the one who condemns? No one. Christ Jesus who died—more than that, who was raised to life—is at the right hand of God and is also interceding for us. Who shall separate us from the love of Christ? Shall trouble or hardship or persecution or famine or nakedness or danger or sword? As it is written:

"For your sake we face death all day long; we are considered as sheep to be slaughtered."

No, in all these things we are more than conquerors through him who loved us. For I am convinced that neither death nor life, neither angels nor demons, neither the present nor the future, nor any powers, neither height nor depth, nor anything else in all creation, will be able to separate us from the love of God that is in Christ Jesus our Lord.

Near the conclusion of that letter in which we find those wonderfully jaw-dropping words, Paul encourages the believers with these words...

<u>*Romans 16:20a*</u> *– The God of peace will soon crush Satan under your feet.*

Wait a minute! I thought Jesus already crushed Satan's head. He did. Yet, while Satan's victory will not ever be, he still puts up a fight during his last breaths. Ed Murphy explains, "… in their crushing by Jesus as the Seed of the woman, Satan and his demonic hosts were not annihilated" (212).

In like manner, Millard Erickson wrote …

This κόσμος or evil system is under the control of the devil. We have already noted this in Paul's reference to "the ruler of the kingdom of the air" (Eph. 2:2). John wrote that "the whole world is under the control of the evil one" (1 John 5:19). Just prior to his betrayal Jesus said to his disciples, "the prince of this world is coming" (John 14:30). Behind and in a sense over all the authorities exercising control in the world, there is a far greater power; they are merely his agents, perhaps unwittingly. Satan actually is the ruler of this domain. Thus Satan's offering Jesus all the kingdoms of the world (Matt. 4:8-9) was not idle and exaggerated boasting. These kingdoms lie within his power, although they are not rightfully his and one day will be fully delivered from that control which he now exercises as a usurper. (662)

13

"HOW SHOULD WE LIVE?"

John, the disciple who referred to himself as *"the one who Jesus loved"* could be called the ambassador of love. Love was his theme.

John 3:16 – For God so loved the world that he gave his one and only Son, that whoever believes in him shall not perish but have eternal life.

1 John 2:5 – But if anyone obeys his word, love for God is truly made complete in them. This is how we know we are in him…

1 John 2:10 – Anyone who loves their brother and sister lives in the light, and there is nothing in them to make them stumble.

1 John 3:11 – For this is the message you heard from the beginning: We should love one another.

The ambassador of love provided a concise description of a faithful Christian.

1 John 2:15-17 – Do not love the world or anything in the world. If anyone loves the world, love for the Father is not in them. For everything in the world—the lust of the flesh, the lust of the eyes, and the pride of life—comes not from the Father but from the world. The world and its desires pass away, but whoever does the will of God lives forever.

As we have established, we live in a broken world that is ruled (temporarily) by Satan. We have established, also, that despite those two truths, great hope exists based on promises from God.

John 16:33 – *"I have told you these things, so that in me you may have peace. In this world you will have trouble. But take heart! I have overcome the world."*

Considering the bad news and good news (gospel) how should we live? We would not be incorrect if we answered with the words of Jesus.

Matthew 22:37-39 – *" 'Love the Lord your God with all your heart and with all your soul and with all your mind.' This is the first and greatest commandment. And the second is like it: 'Love your neighbor as yourself.'"*

Using Jesus' two-part call upon those who choose to follow Him as the guiding starting point, we do well to devote time to learning about ways in which we can live that will reflect devotion to God and His ways. I identify them as Five Life Commitments:

1. Living in The Ordinary Way

2. Living in The Teaching Way

3. Living in The Micah Way

4. Living in The James Way

5. Living in the Battle-Ready Way

<u>Five Life Commitments:</u>

1. Living in The Ordinary Way –

In my previous book, *The Ordinary Way*, I define and detail such a life. I encourage you to read that for further learning. To live The Ordinary Way is to live in light of the Romans 12:1 text.

Romans 12:1 (MSG) – *So here's what I want you to do, God helping you: Take your everyday, ordinary life—your sleeping, eating, going-to-work, and walking-around life—and place it before God as an offering.*

The first of the Five Life Commitments sets in motion the other four. Living in light of the good news is a daily pursuit. One or two, or even six, days a week will not suffice. Living for God in this Genesis Three World is a calling to full-time, life-long devotion. A.J. Conyers, my late professor, wrote, "To choose against sin in a world system that denies God is to swim upstream in a strong current" (164).

2. Living in The Teaching Way --

Matthew 28:18-20 (MSG) – Jesus, undeterred, went right ahead and gave his charge: "God authorized and commanded me to commission you: Go out and train everyone you meet, far and near, in this way of life, marking them by baptism in the threefold name: Father, Son, and Holy Spirit. Then instruct them in the practice of all I have commanded you. I'll be with you as you do this, day after day after day, right up to the end of the age."

Those words, commonly known as The Great Commission, were first spoken to the eleven remaining apostles. Evangelical Christians understand those words to apply to each modern-day Jesus follower. Not all believers are called to be missionaries, as in the move to an unknown place fashion, or to be preachers, as in the stand behind the pulpit / on the stage type, or to be evangelists, as in shouting from street corners; but each believer is to live in such a way that they draw people to Jesus.

John 13:35 – "By this everyone will know that you are my disciples, if you love one another."

1 Peter 3:15 – But in your hearts revere Christ as Lord. Always be prepared to give an answer to everyone who asks you to give the reason for the hope that you have. But do this with gentleness and respect ...

Acts 1:8 – "But you will receive power when the Holy Spirit comes on you; and you will be my witnesses in Jerusalem, and in all Judea and Samaria, and to the ends of the earth."

3. Living in The Micah Way –

Micah 6:8 – He has shown you, O mortal, what is good. And what does the LORD require of you? To act justly and to love mercy and to walk humbly with your God.

In this Genesis Three World, much injustice, cruelty, and boastfulness exist. Those who choose to live in light of the good news are called to pursue and spread justice, mercy, and humility.

How does one pursue and spread justice?

By acting justly. Acting justly refers to courts of law as well as classrooms of study and homes of living. Acting justly is seen in a judge passing a just sentence. Acting justly is seen in a teacher grading fairly and correcting lovingly. Acting justly is seen in a mother who listens, a father who does not provoke, in a marriage treated with honor and respect.

Bryan Stevenson, the executive director of the Equal Justice Initiative which he founded, makes it his life's calling to help win justice for the poor, the people of color, and wrongfully convicted prisoners. His book, which has been adapted into film, tells the story of Walter McMillan who was sentenced in court to the death penalty. *Just Mercy: A Story of Justice and Redemption* was a #1 New York Times Bestseller. Readers (and later, movie goers) enjoyed learning about McMillan's story. One reason they did so is because God wired us to love justice. While we are not great at loving it, we do know justice when we see it.

Psalm 82:3-4 – Defend the weak and the fatherless; uphold the cause of the poor and the oppressed. Rescue the weak and the needy; deliver them from the hand of the wicked.

How does one pursue and spread mercy?

By loving mercy. Loving mercy refers to withholding shame and even rightfully-earned punishment. Loving mercy is seen in a friend who forgives a cruel insult. Loving mercy is seen in a spouse committing to work on rebuilding trust. Loving mercy is seen in a church reaching out to the incarcerated. Loving mercy is seen in forgiving the debt.

The Axis power German pilot, Franz Stigler, received orders from his superiors to kill the enemies, the Allies. Certainly, he followed those orders just as soldiers most often do. But on December 20, 1943, Stigler chose mercy. German fighters shot down an American B-17 piloted by Lieutenant Charlie Brown (real name). Viewing the badly damaged plane, Stigler saw Brown in desperate attempts at landing the wounded bird safely. Stigler chose mercy. He guided Brown to neutral territory and, therefore, life. The merciful act and later meeting were detailed at length in a book by Adam Makos and Larry Alexander. It was also mentioned in Lt. Col. Charles Brown's obituary.

> *At age 21 on his first mission as pilot in command, his plane was badly damaged by German fighters and flack; he and six of his crew were wounded. Upon limping back to England, they were intercepted by yet another enemy fighter over Germany. Recognizing their helpless state, the German pilot did not shoot them down but signaled Charlie to land, surrender and be taken prisoner. In the face of certain death Charlie refused two such demands because his crew needed critical medical care. The chivalrous German pilot, recognizing the courage of his fellow airman, escorted the crippled bomber to the coast, pointed a compass heading to England and saluted his adversary. Forty-five years later the two pilots were re-united and became as close as brothers. Their story continues to receive international acclaim. The chivalrous German pilot, Luftwaffe Ace Franz Stigler passed away on March 22, 2008. (legacy.com)*

From 1990 until their deaths in 2008, Brown and Stigler remained friends.

Matthew 5:7 – Blessed are the merciful, for they will be shown mercy.

How does one pursue and spread humility?

By walking humbly. Walking humbly refers to a forsaking of pride and personal privilege. Walking humbly is seen in the athlete who wins without boasting and loses without sulking. Walking humbly is seen in sharing the platform. Walking humbly is seen in seeking public office without disparaging one's opponent. Walking humbly is seen in saying "How can I help?" instead of "What an idiot!" Walking humbly is seen in couples submitting *"to one another out of reverence for Christ"* (Ephesians 5:21). Thomas Tarrants wrote …

Pride is a universal human problem. Everyone suffers from it to some degree. When we have exalted ourselves in pride, God does not want to punish us and bring us low but rather to forgive and restore us. He says again and again in Scripture, humble yourselves, and I will exalt you. This gives us hope and encouragement. God takes pleasure in our efforts to humble ourselves, and he loves to bless and exalt the humble. For just as pride is the root of all sin, so "humility is the root, mother, nurse, foundation, and bond of all virtue," as John Chrysostom once remarked.

To relay a story of humility seems odd since those who act humbly seek no attention. Nevertheless, even the humble can receive some credit.

In April of 2012, Joyce Hilda Banda was sworn in as President of Malawi. She was the first female president in southern Africa. Upon taking office and seeing the plight of her fellow Malawians, President Banda "sold off the Presidential jet and the fleet of 60 Mercedes limousines to help her country's falling economy" (Archana).

Philippians 2:3-4 – Do nothing out of selfish ambition or vain conceit. Rather, in humility value others above yourselves, not looking to your own interests but each of you to the interests of the others.

James 4:6-10 But he gives us more grace. That is why Scripture says: "God opposes the proud but shows favor to the humble."

Submit yourselves, then, to God. Resist the devil, and he will flee from you. Come near to God and he will come near to you. Wash your hands, you sinners, and purify your hearts, you double-minded. Grieve, mourn and wail. Change your laughter to mourning and your joy to gloom. Humble yourselves before the Lord, and he will lift you up.

4. Living in the James Way –

If John, the apostle of Jesus, can be known as the Ambassador of Love, then perhaps James, the brother of Jesus, can be known as the Ambassador of Deeds. (I'll have more to say about James in the next several chapters.)

James 1:22 – Do not merely listen to the word, and so deceive yourselves. Do what it says.

James 2:14-20 – What good is it, my brothers and sisters, if someone claims to have faith but has no deeds? Can such faith save them? Suppose a brother or a sister is without clothes and daily food. If one of you says to them, "Go in peace; keep warm and well fed," but does nothing about their physical needs, what good is it? In the same way, faith by itself, if it is not accompanied by action, is dead.

But someone will say, "You have faith; I have deeds."

Show me your faith without deeds, and I will show you my faith by my deeds. You believe that there is one God. Good! Even the demons believe that—and shudder.

You foolish person, do you want evidence that faith without deeds is useless?

James was a proof-in-the-pudding type of guy. If the first century held board meetings, James surely skipped them. James calls us to action. He did not disagree with Paul about the centrality of grace; he did his best to warn against misuse of that grace. We learn some key lessons on discipleship from James. I list them in one word each.

Rejoice (1:2)	Welcome (2:1)	Resist (4:7)
Persevere (1:4)	Love (2:8)	Come (4:8)
Ask (1:5)	Speak (2:12)	Endure (5:7)
Note (1:19)	Tame (3:7-8)	Pray (5:13)
Listen (1:19)	Praise (3:9)	Confess (5:16)
Do (1:22)	Submit (4:7)	Remember (5:20)

5. Living in The Battle-Ready-Way – The Prince of Peace, knowing that peace does not yet reign, prepares His followers for battle.

Ephesians 6:10-17 – Finally, be strong in the Lord and in his mighty power. Put on the full armor of God, so that you can take your stand against the devil's schemes. For our struggle is not against flesh and blood, but against the rulers, against the authorities, against the powers of this dark world and against the spiritual forces of evil in the heavenly realms. Therefore put on the full armor of God, so that when the day of evil comes, you may be able to stand your ground, and after you have done everything, to stand. Stand firm then, with the belt of truth buckled around your waist, with the breastplate of righteousness in place, and with your feet fitted with the readiness that comes from the gospel of peace. In addition to all this, take up the shield of faith, with which you can extinguish all the flaming arrows of the evil one. Take the helmet of salvation and the sword of the Spirit, which is the word of God.

Jewish theologian Nahum Sarna wrote… "Man's disobedience is the cause of the human predicament. Human freedom can be at one and the same time an omen of disaster and a challenge and opportunity." (28)

Life in the Genesis Three World is full of disaster and opportunity. Believers can experience more of the latter when they suit up in the full armor of God.

Macho-Christianity teaches Christians – men in particular – to charge into battle against the evil one.

Passive-Christianity suggests that simply biding time as one waits for Jesus' second coming is the wise path.

The former aims to conquer; the latter shoots for a technique of staying quiet and hoping no one notices. Both miss the mark. Ephesians' soldier seeks no battle but is nevertheless prepared for one. The soldier, neither macho or passive, stands firm and prepared by …

- Bible reading (belt of truth)

- Right living (breastplate of righteousness)

- Peace-loving and truth-sharing (feet fitted with readiness)

Romans 10:15 – And how can anyone preach unless they are sent? As it is written: "How beautiful are the feet of those who bring good news!"

- Believing (shield of faith)

- Assurance (helmet of salvation)

- Armed (sword of the Spirit)

14

"JOY IN TRIALS"

As we consider the question of how to live well in the Genesis Three World, we can learn much from James, the brother of Jesus. This chapter and the following six will focus on the wisdom found in James' writing as found in the New Testament.

The student of Scripture meets James for the first time in the thirteenth chapter of Matthew.

> *Matthew 13:55-56a - "Isn't this the carpenter's son? Isn't his mother's name Mary, and aren't his brothers James, Joseph, Simon and Judas? Aren't all his sisters with us?"*

While Joseph and Mary did not conceive Jesus, they did add to His number. Jesus had four brothers and an unknown number of sisters. One of his siblings was James, the writer of the letter of our focus. While during the gospel accounts, James' legacy is not of much significance and spotted with less than stellar example-setting, Jesus' brother was no lost cause. He matured into a key leader in the body of believers in Jerusalem. He grew into a strong leader of firm conviction.

As James sat down to pen the epistle that bears his name, he followed the Holy Spirit's lead and wrote pastoral words to Jews who believed in Jesus as Lord. In this chapter we will focus on the first twelve verses of James' letter.

> *James 1:1-12 – James, a servant of God and of the Lord Jesus Christ, To the twelve tribes scattered among the nations: Greetings. Consider it pure joy, my brothers and sisters, whenever you face trials of many kinds, because you know that the testing of your faith produces perseverance. Let perseverance finish its work*

so that you may be mature and complete, not lacking anything. If any of you lacks wisdom, you should ask God, who gives generously to all without finding fault, and it will be given to you. But when you ask, you must believe and not doubt, because the one who doubts is like a wave of the sea, blown and tossed by the wind. That person should not expect to receive anything from the Lord. Such a person is double-minded and unstable in all they do.

Believers in humble circumstances ought to take pride in their high position. But the rich should take pride in their humiliation— since they will pass away like a wild flower. For the sun rises with scorching heat and withers the plant; its blossom falls and its beauty is destroyed. In the same way, the rich will fade away even while they go about their business.

Blessed is the one who perseveres under trial because, having stood the test, that person will receive the crown of life that the Lord has promised to those who love him.

James writes to scattered people. Because of Roman oppression, thousands of Jews were dispersed all around the lands surrounding the Mediterranean Sea. James sent them words of encouragement and pastoral direction. James has been called the practical theologian. As James Adamson wrote,

"James is addressing people who are supposed to know the rudiments of Christianity; and his aim, as in the Sermon on the Mount, is to set forth the theonomic life in its essentials, that is, life lived according to God's Law." (20)

Immediately upon concluding his words of introduction, James wastes no time in providing pastoral counsel.

James 1:2-11 – Consider it pure joy, my brothers and sisters, whenever you face trials of many kinds, because you know that the testing of your faith produces perseverance. Let perseverance finish its work so that you may be mature and complete, not

lacking anything. If any of you lacks wisdom, you should ask God, who gives generously to all without finding fault, and it will be given to you. But when you ask, you must believe and not doubt, because the one who doubts is like a wave of the sea, blown and tossed by the wind. That person should not expect to receive anything from the Lord. Such a person is double-minded and unstable in all they do.

Believers in humble circumstances ought to take pride in their high position. But the rich should take pride in their humiliation—since they will pass away like a wild flower. For the sun rises with scorching heat and withers the plant; its blossom falls and its beauty is destroyed. In the same way, the rich will fade away even while they go about their business.

James jumps rather than tiptoes into pastoral counsel. In verses two through eight, the brother of Jesus speaks to the often experienced and never welcomed trials of life. The Greek word for "trials" here is peirasmos. It has been translated as trials, temptations, hardships, and other ways. Adamson translates the idea well as, *"trying assaults of evil" (52).*

We live in a Genesis Three World where evil exists. And until Jesus returns, Satan, the prince of darkness, is constantly at work producing, crafting, and encouraging evil.

James does not tell the believers to run and hide. Far from it. He tells them to persevere. How does that work? How, in other words, can we "consider it pure joy"? We find the answer in the flow of the text. Before we find the answer of *How*, let us address the *What*. What does the experience of facing "trying assaults of evil" provide?

James 1:2-4 — Consider it pure joy, my brothers and sisters, whenever you face trials of many kinds, because you know that the testing of your faith produces perseverance. Let perseverance finish its work so that you may be mature and complete, not lacking anything.

1) Perseverance – You will need the on-the-trial training because you will continue to experience trials. Right before Jesus provides the beautiful encouraging words "I have overcome the world" He spoke a difficult truth.

> *John 16:33 – "I have told you these things, so that in me you may have peace. In this world you will have trouble. But take heart! I have overcome the world."*

You will have trouble; learn to face it through perseverance.

2) Maturity – Trials produce perseverance. Collected perseverance builds the muscle of maturity. Teenagers know all too well the feeling of growing pains. Bodybuilders accept that the gains they seek will require regular soreness. Students know that tests and essays require work and that the study for those assignments enhances their learning.

Think now of some lessons you learned through trial. If you handled them well, you grew in maturity.

The experience of assaults of evil produces perseverance and maturity. That is the *What*. Now back to the *How*. How can we consider it pure joy?

> *James 1:5-8 – If any of you lacks wisdom, you should ask God, who gives generously to all without finding fault, and it will be given to you. But when you ask, you must believe and not doubt, because the one who doubts is like a wave of the sea, blown and tossed by the wind. That person should not expect to receive anything from the Lord. Such a person is double-minded and unstable in all they do.*

How can we consider the facing of trials pure joy? By navigating trials with wisdom. We need wisdom. We need the wisdom of Christ. You will never be able to face trials with joy without thinking like Christ. So, what to do?

> *James 1:5 – If any of you lacks wisdom, you should ask God, who gives generously to all without finding fault, and it will be given to you.*

Ask for wisdom and the generous God will grant it. He gives freely. When we ask, we need to ask in belief. Such confident asking displays our trust in our King.

As we wait expectantly for wisdom of the King we must do so in humility. Hear James.

James 1:9-11 – Believers in humble circumstances ought to take pride in their high position. But the rich should take pride in their humiliation—since they will pass away like a wild flower. For the sun rises with scorching heat and withers the plant; its blossom falls and its beauty is destroyed. In the same way, the rich will fade away even while they go about their business.

Rich and poor alike need to humble themselves in the sight of God as they seek wisdom. James leans more heavily into the wealthy because it is often more difficult for those with much to realize how much need they really have. It is too easy to trust in money due to its power to accomplish much. However, as many wealthy people will attest, money never buys true wisdom. Stuff, yes. Toys, yes. Comfort, yes. Wisdom? No!

Having stated his case James restates his conviction.

James 1:12 – Blessed is the one who perseveres under trial because, having stood the test, that person will receive the crown of life that the Lord has promised to those who love him.

Pure joy is attainable through wisdom which provides us with the right mind through which we can face trials well. Notice a truth. Joy requires action. You and I do not simply experience joy during trials. We must seek joy and work at it to bring it into reality. When you do that, you will find true joy.

Let us not be confused. James is not telling us to be glad that evil occurs or that pain is part of our reality. Rather he teaches us to consider it all joy even as we look forward to the day when Christ will welcome us into Eternity. We can consider it joy because we know that in our trials we are not alone and that our trials do not have the last word. Jesus does!

15

"DO WHAT IT SAYS"

In verses thirteen through eighteen of the first chapter of James, he teaches two main points.

1. God does not tempt us. Gone are the excuses that our mistakes are in any way God's fault. We must take ownership.

2. God gives generously and is forever consistent and faithful. In the words of David Nystrom,

"Remember that God is trustworthy and wholly good, and this will sustain you in the midst of any difficulty" (78).

With those two main points stated, James, having addressed the nature of trials and the call on believers to find joy during them, turns to another subject. We could call the next section the "Proof in the Pudding" section. James explains the telling proof of true faith.

James 1:19-27 My dear brothers and sisters, take note of this: Everyone should be quick to listen, slow to speak and slow to become angry, because human anger does not produce the righteousness that God desires. Therefore, get rid of all moral filth and the evil that is so prevalent and humbly accept the word planted in you, which can save you.

Do not merely listen to the word, and so deceive yourselves. Do what it says. Anyone who listens to the word but does not do what it says is like someone who looks at his face in a mirror and, after looking at himself, goes away and immediately forgets what he looks like. But whoever looks intently into the perfect law that gives freedom, and continues in it—not forgetting what they have heard, but doing it—they will be blessed in what they do.

Those who consider themselves religious and yet do not keep a tight rein on their tongues deceive themselves, and their religion is worthless. Religion that God our Father accepts as pure and faultless is this: to look after orphans and widows in their distress and to keep oneself from being polluted by the world.

James is a great advocate for grace. Remember his words during The Council in Jerusalem where it was decided that Gentile believers did not need to be burdened with Jewish law.

Acts 15:19 – "It is my judgment, therefore, that we should not make it difficult for the Gentiles who are turning to God."

Grace, to James, however, did not allow for an action-less faith. He addresses that in the third chapter, but he starts addressing it here. Join me in unpacking his divinely-inspired argument. I will break his words down into smaller sections that we can address one-by-one.

1. Avoid Anger

James 1:19-20 – My dear brothers and sisters, take note of this: Everyone should be quick to listen, slow to speak and slow to become angry, because human anger does not produce the righteousness that God desires.

James provides words that remind us to regulate our speed. He calls us to be quick.

<u>Be quick to listen.</u>
Much anger arises unnecessarily because of misunderstanding. So often such misunderstanding is the result of failure to listen. We jump to conclusions. We fill in and finish sentences with assumed rather than heard words.

James calls us to be quick to listen; he also calls us to be slow.

<u>Be slow to speak.</u>

As a Jew by birth, James was a student of the Hebrew Scriptures. He knew the words of Proverbs. Listen to two of them.

Proverbs 18:2 – Fools find no pleasure in understanding but delight in airing their own opinions.

Proverbs 18:13 – To answer before listening—that is folly and shame.

Fools speak too soon. We must listen before we speak. Consider the words you wish you had never spoken. You will have less to undo if you will listen to James and be slow to speak.

<u>Be slow to become angry.</u>

When you commit to quick listening and slow speaking, you will get a firm grip on your anger. That firm grip will inhibit the rapid flying off the handle.

2. Accept and do the word

James 1:21-25 – Therefore, get rid of all moral filth and the evil that is so prevalent and humbly accept the word planted in you, which can save you.

Do not merely listen to the word, and so deceive yourselves. Do what it says. Anyone who listens to the word but does not do what it says is like someone who looks at his face in a mirror and, after looking at himself, goes away and immediately forgets what he looks like. But whoever looks intently into the perfect law that gives freedom, and continues in it—not forgetting what they have heard, but doing it—they will be blessed in what they do.

In verse 18, 21, and 22, James mentions <u>the word</u>. He refers to it as "the word of truth," "the word planted in you," and simply "the word." He is referring to Scripture and particularly the Gospel. He urges his readers to accept and live the good news of Jesus. The Jewish people thought of the

Torah (Law) as the medicine of life. We need the word within us to make us well and to be well.

Once we accept the truth of the good news, we need to do some housecleaning.

> *James 1:21 – Therefore, get rid of all moral filth and the evil that is so prevalent and humbly accept the word planted in you, which can save you.*

As you strive to live the word, you need to make space for the filling of your life. You make more space by getting rid of moral filth and evil. What filth and evil are in your life that you need to throw away? Greed? Sexual sin? Pornography? Wishing harm on another? Poor choices in entertainment (music, movies, books, etc.)? Listen to the list of filth mentioned by Paul.

> *Ephesians 5:3-8 – But among you there must not be even a hint of sexual immorality, or of any kind of impurity, or of greed, because these are improper for God's holy people. Nor should there be obscenity, foolish talk or coarse joking, which are out of place, but rather thanksgiving. For of this you can be sure: No immoral, impure or greedy person—such a person is an idolater—has any inheritance in the kingdom of Christ and of God. Let no one deceive you with empty words, for because of such things God's wrath comes on those who are disobedient. Therefore, do not be partners with them. For you were once darkness, but now you are light in the Lord. Live as children of light*

When we hear the words of James and Paul, which were – remember – inspired by God, we need to do what they say. If we do not, we are like the one who looks in the mirror and then forgets the image of themselves. Think about that analogy this way. We've all experienced it. You hear from God through a sermon on Sunday or reading the Bible during the week and you know that God is calling you to make a life change. Then you walk out the door of the church or into another room of your house having done nothing about the call God gave you. Do not merely listen to God. Do what He says.

3. Do what the word says in specific ways.

> *James 1:26-27 – Those who consider themselves religious and yet do not keep a tight rein on their tongues deceive themselves, and their religion is worthless. Religion that God our Father accepts as pure and faultless is this: to look after orphans and widows in their distress and to keep oneself from being polluted by the world.*

Water-tight theology, ceremonial rites, purity rituals, and the like are not central. What James is saying is that we need to possess a faith that exhibits a commitment to living the Great Commandment.

- Love God

- Love People

James provides examples of how to do that. The first is to rein in our tongues. I will save more discussion on that because James will hit that theme hard in chapter three. The second example James provides is the care of orphans and widows. Hear again from the Proverbs James knew so well.

> *Proverbs 14:31 - Whoever oppresses the poor shows contempt for their Maker, but whoever is kind to the needy honors God.*

In the first century, as is often the case today, orphans and widows were among the poor. James Adamson reminds us cleverly that, "The Fatherhood of God implies the brotherhood of man" (86).

As believers, we are siblings, as are all people God created. James tells siblings to take care of each other, especially those who are in great need.

The third example James gives is summarized in but a few words. *"Keep oneself from being polluted by the world."*

Through the knowledge gained from Scripture, the teaching received in the community of faith, and the direction of the Holy Spirit, we are to keep our ways pure.

As we have witnessed, James' first chapter is filled with calls to action. I encourage you to read carefully and slowly through the text of James 1:19-27 and listen. Then, do what it says.

Mark T. Goodman, DMin.

16

"NO FAVORITES"

Simon Peter, of Hebrew birth, walked into the home of Cornelius, a Roman Gentile, and spoke to a crowd of people about a truth, which he, himself, did not grasp until the God-sent sheet full of "unclean animals" appeared to him in a roof-top vision. He said, "I now realize how true it is that God does not show favoritism." (Acts 10:34)

Paul, the apostle, of Hebrew birth and from relative wealth wrote to a church conflicted by the argument of how to have standing before God. He wrote,

Galatians 3:26-28 – So in Christ Jesus you are all children of God through faith, for all of you who were baptized into Christ have clothed yourselves with Christ. There is neither Jew nor Gentile, neither slave nor free, nor is there male and female, for you are all one in Christ Jesus.

God shows no one favoritism. Christ died for all. Jew, Gentile, Slave, Free, Male, Female, and let us not forget Rich and Poor. That last unnecessary and hurtful divide proved to be one of the most difficult to release from a habitual cling. James, the brother of Jesus, refused to let the issue go unaddressed. We pick up where we left off in the last chapter and find James' address.

James 2:1-13 – My brothers and sisters, believers in our glorious Lord Jesus Christ must not show favoritism. Suppose a man comes into your meeting wearing a gold ring and fine clothes, and a poor man in filthy old clothes also comes in. If you show special attention to the man wearing fine clothes and say, "Here's a good seat for you," but say to the poor man, "You stand there" or "Sit on the floor by my feet," have you not discriminated among yourselves and become judges with evil thoughts?

Listen, my dear brothers and sisters: Has not God chosen those who are poor in the eyes of the world to be rich in faith and to inherit the kingdom he promised those who love him? But you have dishonored the poor. Is it not the rich who are exploiting you? Are they not the ones who are dragging you into court? Are they not the ones who are blaspheming the noble name of him to whom you belong?

If you really keep the royal law found in Scripture, "Love your neighbor as yourself," you are doing right. But if you show favoritism, you sin and are convicted by the law as lawbreakers. For whoever keeps the whole law and yet stumbles at just one point is guilty of breaking all of it. For he who said, "You shall not commit adultery," also said, "You shall not murder." If you do not commit adultery but do commit murder, you have become a lawbreaker.

Speak and act as those who are going to be judged by the law that gives freedom, because judgment without mercy will be shown to anyone who has not been merciful. Mercy triumphs over judgment.

Within these words we read warning, reminders, and calls to action. Join me in discovering those. To do so, I want to draw your attention to four key observations from the text.

1) We are to show no favoritism.

There are multiple phrases in the Greek (original language) of this text that refer to favoritism. One is from the same root word as found in Acts 10:34. It is often translated as "respecter of persons." The other Greek term is epiblépō (ἐπιβλέπω). Epiblépō means to gaze at or lift one's face to.

We understand therefore that we are not to give special attention to persons of wealth. Why would we? Why do we?

- to show respect so that we are thought well of

- in hopes that they will be generous with us ("What can I get out of this?")

Notice the parable-of-sorts that James uses.

> *James 2:3-4 – If you show special attention to the man wearing fine clothes and say, "Here's a good seat for you," but say to the poor man, "You stand there" or "Sit on the floor by my feet," have you not discriminated among yourselves and become judges with evil thoughts?*

When I picture this story, I think of a greeter taking the wealthy man to a front row seat. Think a center orchestra seat at the Majestic Theatre in New York City. But then I realize - since the setting is a religious meeting - if it were today, the back row seats would be the most coveted.

Regardless of seat placement, it's the best seat in the house for the rich ring-fingered man and the floor for the poor man.

Several years ago, during one of the Sunday worship services of the church where I served at the time, I saw the love of Jesus in the actions of my friend Larry. As I stood on the platform preaching, a man who was homeless, with the appearance and aroma to prove it, entered the sanctuary and sat down on the back pew to listen. I knew the man and was glad to see him. I'll call him "Frank." As Frank listened, he grew tired in the warmth of the room and rather quickly drifted off to sleep. Still, I was glad he was there. While, thankfully, a sleeping listener during my sermons is rare, it does happen. And happen it did that day! Frank's level of sleeping deepened and soon his appearance and aroma were accompanied by loud snoring that echoed throughout the building. I kept preaching but was not sure how well others could listen as snoring at times conquered sermon. Understanding the situation, Larry moved into action. Larry knew the importance of hearing the Word as well as loving one's neighbor. So, Larry left his near-the-front pew and joined Frank on the back pew, providing his shoulder as a pillow for the sleeping man. The adjustment changed the angle of Frank's head and quieted the snoring, enabling the needed rest as well as the needed listening. I know that as Frank slept and the congregation listened, Jesus was pleased.

The people of the church received two sermons that Sunday – one spoken and one lived.

2) God holds a special place in His heart for the poor.

James 2:5 – Listen, my dear brothers and sisters: Has not God chosen those who are poor in the eyes of the world to be rich in faith and to inherit the kingdom he promised those who love him?

I have no information about dollar or salary amounts that would provide a scale for us. What does it mean to be rich? What does it mean to be poor? Truly, it's relative. I've been to many places in the world where I have felt and been wealthy, in relation to the people who live there. I've never felt poor, but I see others and think of them as rich. Very few rich people think they are rich even though nearly all of us are rich compared to much of the world's population. So, don't let yourself off the hook here just yet. James Adamson's words are helpful for our understanding.

Not every rich man is doomed to be damned, and not every poor man is sure to be saved; but for the purposes of this chapter there is a deep difference between the rich, in general, and the poor, in general. (108-109)

We recall the words of Jesus on the matter.

Matthew 19:24 – "Again I tell you, it is easier for a camel to go through the eye of a needle than for someone who is rich to enter the kingdom of God."

Why is that? It is often the case that those who greatly enjoy their wealth have a difficult time realizing the importance of humility as well as seeing their own need for rescue.

It is important to make another observation about God's heart for the poor. While "poor" refers to financial ranking, it encompasses much more.

Matthew 5:3 – "Blessed are the poor in spirit, for theirs is the kingdom of heaven."

Money-poor people can miss out on the blessings of God if they are not poor in spirit, not humble, and not seeking God. The same is true of money-rich people.

3) Neglecting to love the poor is disobedience.

> *James 2:8-11 – If you really keep the royal law found in Scripture, "Love your neighbor as yourself," you are doing right. But if you show favoritism, you sin and are convicted by the law as lawbreakers. For whoever keeps the whole law and yet stumbles at just one point is guilty of breaking all of it. For he who said, "You shall not commit adultery," also said, "You shall not murder." If you do not commit adultery but do commit murder, you have become a lawbreaker.*

We "are doing right" when we love our neighbors (no matter how close or far away they live from us). Loving those neighbors who are like James' poor man means that we treat them as well as we would a man wearing gold rings and fine clothes. James won't let up here. He challenges his readers, telling them (us) that they cannot pick and choose which laws to keep (referring to two of the Ten Commandments). The one who does not love his or her neighbor is just as much a lawbreaker as is the murderer or adulterer.

4) Jesus-followers are to speak and act like it.

> *James 2:12-13 – Speak and act as those who are going to be judged by the law that gives freedom, because judgment without mercy will be shown to anyone who has not been merciful. Mercy triumphs over judgment.*

Within verse twelve, we see James' reference to "the law that gives freedom." The law to which he refers is the second of the great commandments. Return to verse 8.

<u>James 2:8</u> – If you really keep the royal law found in Scripture, "Love your neighbor as yourself," you are doing right.

True believers understand the utter necessity of loving our neighbors in our speech and with our actions. One sure sign that we are doing that is when we show and extend mercy. James warns the merciless that they too will receive no mercy.

Poverty is a complex issue within our society. I do not have the answer to fixing the problem. Indeed, Jesus tells us that the poor will always be among us. Yet, that does not allow us to see only the big socioeconomic problem and therefore do nothing. You and I cannot show love to all the "poor," but we can show love to a poor person. We can even show love to a great number of people in poverty one person at a time.

As I read Adamson, I came across a powerfully challenging sentence. "Do not try to combine faith in the Lord Jesus Christ, our Glory, with worship of men's social status" (101). Recall Jesus' response to the question about the most important part of the O.T. Law.

<u>Mark 12:30-31</u> – "'Love the Lord your God with all your heart and with all your soul and with all your mind and with all your strength.' The second is this: 'Love your neighbor as yourself.' There is no commandment greater than these."

Jesus connected the two for a reason. You cannot have one without the other. If you truly love the Lord your God, you will love your neighbor. Remember to love all your neighbors regardless of what they are wearing - fine clothes or filthy clothes.

17

"SHOW ME FAITH"

In 1899, Willard Vandiver, the Congressman from Missouri, doubted the truth of a speaker who proceeded him and therefore said,

I come from a state that raises corn and cotton and cockleburs and Democrats, and frothy eloquence neither convinces nor satisfies me. I am from Missouri. You have got to show me. (qtd in The State of Missouri).

To this day, the unofficial motto of the state of Missouri is "The Show Me State."

Following suit, we could refer to the one who wrote our biblical book of focus for this series of chapters as "The Show Me Man."

- James advocated for action.

- James rallied for results.

- James demanded deeds.

James 2:14-26 – What good is it, my brothers and sisters, if someone claims to have faith but has no deeds? Can such faith save them? Suppose a brother or a sister is without clothes and daily food. If one of you says to them, "Go in peace; keep warm and well fed," but does nothing about their physical needs, what good is it? In the same way, faith by itself, if it is not accompanied by action, is dead.

But someone will say, "You have faith; I have deeds."

Show me your faith without deeds, and I will show you my faith by my deeds. You believe that there is one God. Good! Even the demons believe that—and shudder.

You foolish person, do you want evidence that faith without deeds is useless? Was not our father Abraham considered righteous for what he did when he offered his son Isaac on the altar? You see that his faith and his actions were working together, and his faith was made complete by what he did. And the scripture was fulfilled that says, "Abraham believed God, and it was credited to him as righteousness," and he was called God's friend. You see that a person is considered righteous by what they do and not by faith alone.

In the same way, was not even Rahab the prostitute considered righteous for what she did when she gave lodging to the spies and sent them off in a different direction? As the body without the spirit is dead, so faith without deeds is dead.

According to statisticians, as of the year 2020, approximately 2.38 billion people are Christians. If James were here today, he would disagree. While it is not our responsibility to state or determine who is and who is not a Christian, we, according to James, can at least know about ourselves regarding the authenticity of our faith. Before we unpack James' words, let us revisit some of the most well-known words in the Bible.

John 3:16 – For God so loved the world that he gave his one and only Son, that whoever believes in him shall not perish but have eternal life.

Within that powerful and life-altering verse, we learn the requirement for eternal life with God—belief in Jesus. Unfortunately, due to poorly explained word meaning, a great number of evangelicals have reduced the meaning of "believe" to a mere intellectual and emotional consent. As in "I cognitively acknowledge Jesus' existence and feel the need to accept Him." Hear me! That's a good start. That type of belief, however, is not complete.

John Sammis said it well in his lyrics to a one hundred- and thirty-five-year-old hymn.

"Trust and Obey"
When we walk with the Lord
In the light of His word
What a glory he sheds on our way;
While we do His good will,
He abides with us still,
And with all who will trust and obey.
Trust and obey,
For there's no other way
To be happy in Jesus,
But to trust and obey.

To believe in Jesus is to trust Jesus and obey Jesus. We, if we are true Christians, will do both.

The perversion of Christian teaching which James attacks is the notion that a confession of faith guarantees salvation regardless of the conduct of the believer; in other words, that the recital of a creed makes a man acceptable to God despite his behavior toward his fellows. (Poteat 40)

Hear James.

James 2:22 – You see that his faith and his actions were working together, and his faith was made complete by what he did.

James shows that faith "is indissolubly linked to works, neither being unduly stressed at the expense of the other" (Adamson 129). Some churches over-emphasize deeds/works; other churches over-emphasize faith. Neither needs to be unduly stressed.

To help us grasp this, James provides two positive examples of faith and one faulty example.

Positive Examples:

1) Abraham - God issued a call to Abraham to leave his *known* and enter the *unknown*. That move to a new and unfamiliar place, however, was not Abraham's most difficult assignment. Abraham understood God to tell him to take Isaac his son and sacrifice him, rather than a ram, as an offering to the Lord. Thankfully, God stayed Abraham's hand as the servant of God prepared to take a blade to his son. Abraham exemplified faith; Isaac was spared; the message of the need for sacrifice was loud and clear.

James 2:21-23 – Was not our father Abraham considered righteous for what he did when he offered his son Isaac on the altar? You see that his faith and his actions were working together, and his faith was made complete by what he did. And the scripture was fulfilled that says, "Abraham believed God, and it was credited to him as righteousness," and he was called God's friend.

2) Rahab - Forty years of wilderness wandering was coming to an end. Moses, God's servant who was now dead, had entrusted his role of leader to Joshua. Joshua had his own Red Sea moment as he led the next generation of Israelites on dry ground to the land of promise. The land of promise was not up for sale or unoccupied. To enjoy the milk and honey of the land, they needed possession of it; in order to have possession, they needed to defeat and displace (and sometimes kill) the people who called the land their home. The most notable victory occurred in a town known as Jericho. In Jericho lived a woman who practiced a profession nearly as old as history itself. As she was accustomed to welcoming men into her home, Rahab the prostitute allowed the Hebrew spies to stay in here home, yet they entered for no nefarious purpose. They entered to seek refuge. Rahab saved their mission and their lives.

James 2:25 – In the same way, was not even Rahab the prostitute considered righteous for what she did when she gave lodging to the spies and sent them off in a different direction?

Negative Example: Demons

James 2:19 – You believe that there is one God. Good! Even the demons believe that—and shudder.

Many Christians struggle with James. In fact, Martin Luther, the great church reformer, famously argued against the book of James' rightful place in the biblical canon. Why? Because they hear more from Paul than James. For example ...

Ephesians 2:8-9 – For it is by grace you have been saved, through faith—and this is not from yourselves, it is the gift of God—not by works, so that no one can boast.

We believe the Bible is true and unified. How then can Paul and James be in the same Bible? It is important to note here that Paul primarily wrote to people who were trying to work their way into heaven. He, therefore, highly and primarily promoted faith. He did not, however, neglect a call to deeds.

Galatians 5:13-17 You, my brothers and sisters, were called to be free. But do not use your freedom to indulge the flesh; rather, serve one another humbly in love. For the entire law is fulfilled in keeping this one command: "Love your neighbor as yourself." If you bite and devour each other, watch out or you will be destroyed by each other.

So, I say, walk by the Spirit, and you will not gratify the desires of the flesh. For the flesh desires what is contrary to the Spirit, and the Spirit what is contrary to the flesh. They are in conflict with each other, so that you are not to do whatever you want.

James promotes deeds without neglecting faith. Paul promotes faith without neglecting deeds. For good reason their writings are in one unified Bible. We need to hear and heed both men.

That truth raises an interesting question.

Do you relate more to James or Paul?

If James, then I offer you these reminders.

1. You have the desire to do deeds because of God.

2. While God delights in your works, He is not impressed by them.

3. Faith is not a contest.

4. You will not and cannot earn your way into heaven.

If Paul, then I offer you these reminders.

1. You have a strong faith because of God.

2. God calls you to trust and obey, not just to trust.

3. Deeds are essential to faith.

4. God has things for you to do before you get to heaven.

Christianity is a "Show Me" faith.

James 2:26 – *As the body without the spirit is dead, so faith without deeds is dead.*

18

"LIKE BITLESS HORSES"

Let's face it -- English is a crazy language. There is no egg in eggplant nor ham in hamburger; neither apple nor pine in pineapple. English muffins weren't invented in England really? or French fries in France. Sweetmeats are candies while sweetbreads, which aren't sweet, are meat.

We take English for granted. But if we explore its paradoxes, we find that quicksand can work slowly, boxing rings are square and a guinea pig is neither from Guinea nor is it a pig.

And why is it that writers write but fingers don't fing, grocers don't groce and hammers don't ham? If the plural of tooth is teeth, why isn't the plural of booth beeth? One goose, 2 geese. So one moose, 2 meese? One index, 2 indices?

Doesn't it seem crazy that you can make amends but not one amend, that you comb through annals of history but not a single annal? If you have a bunch of odds and ends and get rid of all but one of them, what do you call it?

If teachers taught, why didn't preacher praught? If a vegetarian eats vegetables, what does a humanitarian eat? If you wrote a letter, perhaps you bote your tongue? (Lederer)

The English language can be crazily frustrating, so can our lack of self-control with our use of it.

You know the struggle.

- You praise Jesus as you sing in church; and on your way home, curse the lazy driver who won't move to the right lane.

- You say "I love you" in the morning yet scream out threats that evening.

- You promise to be home for dinner only to heat the leftovers when you eventually arrive.

- You beg for mercy in the classroom and promptly trash your algebra teacher.

In this chapter, we continue our study of the book of James. While James did not speak English, he understood the struggle of control of what we say.

James 3:1-12 Not many of you should become teachers, my fellow believers, because you know that we who teach will be judged more strictly. We all stumble in many ways. Anyone who is never at fault in what they say is perfect, able to keep their whole body in check.

When we put bits into the mouths of horses to make them obey us, we can turn the whole animal. Or take ships as an example. Although they are so large and are driven by strong winds, they are steered by a very small rudder wherever the pilot wants to go. Likewise, the tongue is a small part of the body, but it makes great boasts. Consider what a great forest is set on fire by a small spark. The tongue also is a fire, a world of evil among the parts of the body. It corrupts the whole body, sets the whole course of one's life on fire, and is itself set on fire by hell.

All kinds of animals, birds, reptiles and sea creatures are being tamed and have been tamed by mankind, but no human being can tame the tongue. It is a restless evil, full of deadly poison.

With the tongue we praise our Lord and Father, and with it we curse human beings, who have been made in God's likeness. Out of the same mouth come praise and cursing. My brothers and sisters, this should not be. Can both fresh water and salt water flow from the same spring? My brothers and sisters, can a fig tree bear olives, or a grapevine bear figs? Neither can a salt spring produce fresh water.

James begins this section with a word of caution to any who would strive to teach the Scriptures and thus take on a leadership role within the church.

James 3:1 – Not many of you should become teachers, my fellow believers, because you know that we who teach will be judged more strictly.

We who teach will be judged more strictly. Gordon Poteat explains James' thought well.

His warning was against aiming at the prestige of the teacher's vocation without being aware of this necessary burden. Let no one enter this profession without having his eyes open to the obligation involved therein. (46)

After addressing a topic unique to a few, James spreads his teaching net further out. He mentions the impossibility of perfection and, therefore, the difficulty of keeping one's whole body in check. Then he focuses on one particular body part.

James 3:3-8 – When we put bits into the mouths of horses to make them obey us, we can turn the whole animal. Or take ships as an example. Although they are so large and are driven by strong winds, they are steered by a very small rudder wherever the pilot wants to go. Likewise, the tongue is a small part of the body, but it makes great boasts. Consider what a great forest is set on fire by a small spark. The tongue also is a fire, a world of evil among the parts of the body. It corrupts the whole body, sets the whole course of one's life on fire, and is itself set on fire by hell.

All kinds of animals, birds, reptiles and sea creatures are being tamed and have been tamed by mankind, but no human being can tame the tongue. It is a restless evil, full of deadly poison.

I dare say that very few of you struggled to withhold a punch from a co-worker's face this past week. However, the number increases quite a bit when rather than speaking of throwing punches, I speak of throwing words. Did you speak a careless word to your spouse or discouraging words to your children? Did you allow your anger to unleash your tongue heartlessly on the person just trying to do her job? Notice three words I chose to use in those questions: Careless. Discouraging. Heartlessly.

1. Careless – To speak with less care.

2. Discouraging – To take out rather than to inspire courage.

3. Heartlessly – To use less heart (less love).

You and I know better, yet we often don't do better. Why?
Notice James' analogies.

1) Horses yielding to bits.

2) Boats steered by rudders.

> *Horses and boats are big, but we found ways to control them. Yet the tongue, small as it is, proves more difficult to tame and direct.*

3) A dangerous fire.

The tongue can cause serious damage. We use words such as "roasted" and "burned" in reference to one's victory over another. No wonder!

Just in case we haven't clued into his point yet, James offers other examples—different types of water, vines, and trees. His points?

1. The tongue is difficult to control, but

2. We must learn to control it.

How can we control our tongues?

We can learn much from tools such as Beth Day's poem "Three Gates." In part, Day wrote,

...Make it pass.
> *Before you speak, three gates of gold.*
> *These narrow gates. First, "Is it true?"*

> *Then, "Is it needful?" In your mind*
> *Give truthful answer. And the next*
> *Is last and narrowest, "Is it kind?"*
> *And if to reach your lips at last*
> *It passes through these gateways three,*
> *Then you may tell the tale, nor fear*
> *What the result of speech may be."*

Three gates:

1. Is it true?

2. Is it needful?

3. Is it kind?

As helpful as Day's words are, they are a tool to use after you address the bigger issue. Recall the commandment to love the Lord your God with your all. Your all includes your tongue. Yet let's go deeper; your all includes your heart. Hear Jesus.

> *Luke 6:45 – A good man brings good things out of the good stored up in his heart, and an evil man brings evil things out of the evil stored up in his heart. For the mouth speaks what the heart is full of.*

You will fail to control your heart until you submit your heart to God. Surrender your heart to God and then as the Spirit works in you, you will grow in strength to control your tongue. I encourage you to stay in the Scriptures and allow them to teach you how to do that. Let us look at some examples.

> *Proverbs 15:1 – A gentle answer turns away wrath, but a harsh word stirs up anger.*

> *Proverbs 15:4 – The soothing tongue is a tree of life, but a perverse tongue crushes the spirit.*

Matthew 12:36 – But I tell you that everyone will have to give account on the day of judgment for every empty word they have spoken.

Matthew 15:11 – What goes into someone's mouth does not defile them, but what comes out of their mouth, that is what defiles them.

Ephesians 4:29 – Do not let any unwholesome talk come out of your mouths, but only what is helpful for building others up according to their needs, that it may benefit those who listen.

Ephesians 5:4 – Nor should there be obscenity, foolish talk or coarse joking, which are out of place, but rather thanksgiving.

These six verses are just a sampling of what the Bible teaches us about our use of words. We have much to learn. Returning to our text in James, I will close this chapter with James' weighty observation.

James 3:9-10 – With the tongue we praise our Lord and Father, and with it we curse human beings, who have been made in God's likeness. Out of the same mouth come praise and cursing. My brothers and sisters, this should not be.

19

"KNOWING AND SHOWING"

When God chose to create humans, He placed within them the capacity as well as the desire for thought. Humans, regardless of education level, engage in deep thought to a degree unmatched by any other created beings.

While all humans ponder, those who devote their lives to the academic study of philosophy, dive most deeply into the activity. Indeed, the word philosophy itself is composed of two Greek words meaning "love" and "wisdom". Philosophers are lovers of wisdom. Within the discipline of philosophy is a branch called Ethics or Moral Philosophy. There are three major areas of ethics.

1. Meta-ethics

2. Normative ethics

3. Applied ethics

Meta-ethics asks the question, "What is morality?"
Normative ethics asks the question, "How should we act?"
Applied ethics asks the question, "How do we put morals into practice?"

Keep those areas of ethics in mind as we consider the passage from James which will be the focus of this chapter.

James 3:13-4:17 – Who is wise and understanding among you? Let them show it by their good life, by deeds done in the humility that comes from wisdom. But if you harbor bitter envy and selfish ambition in your hearts, do not boast about it or deny the truth. Such "wisdom" does not come down from heaven but is earthly, unspiritual, demonic. For where you have envy and selfish ambition, there you find disorder and every evil practice.

But the wisdom that comes from heaven is first of all pure; then peace-loving, considerate, submissive, full of mercy and good fruit, impartial and sincere. Peacemakers who sow in peace reap a harvest of righteousness.

What causes fights and quarrels among you? Don't they come from your desires that battle within you? You desire but do not have, so you kill. You covet but you cannot get what you want, so you quarrel and fight. You do not have because you do not ask God. When you ask, you do not receive, because you ask with wrong motives, that you may spend what you get on your pleasures.

You adulterous people, don't you know that friendship with the world means enmity against God? Therefore, anyone who chooses to be a friend of the world becomes an enemy of God. Or do you think Scripture says without reason that he jealously longs for the spirit he has caused to dwell in us? But he gives us more grace. That is why Scripture says: "God opposes the proud but shows favor to the humble."

Submit yourselves, then, to God. Resist the devil, and he will flee from you. Come near to God and he will come near to you. Wash your hands, you sinners, and purify your hearts, you double-minded. Grieve, mourn and wail. Change your laughter to mourning and your joy to gloom. Humble yourselves before the Lord, and he will lift you up.

Brothers and sisters, do not slander one another. Anyone who speaks against a brother or sister or judges them speaks against the law and judges it. When you judge the law, you are not keeping it, but sitting in judgment on it. There is only one Lawgiver and Judge, the one who is able to save and destroy. But you—who are you to judge your neighbor?

Now listen, you who say, "Today or tomorrow we will go to this or that city, spend a year there, carry on business and make money." Why, you do not even know what will happen tomorrow. What is your life? You are a mist that appears for a little while and then vanishes. Instead, you ought to say, "If it is the Lord's will, we will live and do this or that." As it is, you boast in your arrogant schemes. All such boasting is evil. If anyone, then, knows the good they ought to do and doesn't do it, it is sin for them.

Approaching this text through the lens of philosophy we can follow James' argument well.

1. What is the Meta-ethic?

To ask that in a fashion more fitting to the passage: What is the evidence of wisdom?

The Greek word here in James is the same as in the word philosophy—Wisdom is Sophia. James argues that Sophia is shown, not just known.

> *James 3:13 – Who is wise and understanding among you? Let them show it by their good life, by deeds done in the humility that comes from wisdom.*

Eugene Peterson translated that verse in a brilliant fashion.

> *James 3:13 (MSG) – Do you want to be counted wise, to build a reputation for wisdom? Here's what you do: Live well, live wisely, live humbly. It's the way you live, not the way you talk, that counts.*

James, like Jesus before him, saw no way for a person to believe without doing. In fact, he was repulsed by false wisdom. Notice his stern words.

> *James 3:15 – Such "wisdom" does not come down from heaven but is earthly, unspiritual, demonic.*

Christians believe and act.

So, the meta-ethic of this passage is, in summary, wisdom is exhibited in living. It reminds us of James' words from earlier,

James 2:17 – In the same way, faith by itself, if it is not accompanied by action, is dead.

2. What is the Normative ethic?

How should we behave considering the truth that wisdom is exhibited in living? James answers that question.

James 3:17 - 4:6 – But the wisdom that comes from heaven is first of all pure; then peace-loving, considerate, submissive, full of mercy and good fruit, impartial and sincere. Peacemakers who sow in peace reap a harvest of righteousness.

What causes fights and quarrels among you? Don't they come from your desires that battle within you? You desire but do not have, so you kill. You covet but you cannot get what you want, so you quarrel and fight. You do not have because you do not ask God. When you ask, you do not receive, because you ask with wrong motives, that you may spend what you get on your pleasures.

You adulterous people, don't you know that friendship with the world means enmity against God? Therefore, anyone who chooses to be a friend of the world becomes an enemy of God. Or do you think Scripture says without reason that he jealously longs for the spirit he has caused to dwell in us? But he gives us more grace. That is why Scripture says:"God opposes the proud but shows favor to the humble."

First notice the seven attributes of wisdom.

James 3:17 – But the wisdom that comes from heaven is first of all pure; then peace-loving, considerate, submissive, full of mercy and good fruit, impartial and sincere.

The evidence of a life given to wisdom is seen through the presence of these seven attributes. One can know the definition of peace; but if he is not peace-loving, he is not wise. One can know about mercy; but unless she extends mercy, she is not wise.

Next notice the evidence of the lack of wisdom.

James 4:1-4 – What causes fights and quarrels among you? Don't they come from your desires that battle within you? You desire but do not have, so you kill. You covet but you cannot get what you want, so you quarrel and fight. You do not have because you do not ask God. When you ask, you do not receive, because you ask with wrong motives, that you may spend what you get on your pleasures.

You adulterous people, don't you know that friendship with the world means enmity against God? Therefore, anyone who chooses to be a friend of the world becomes an enemy of God.

a) Distorted Desires

b) Wrong Motives

c) Adulterous Behavior

Returning to our question of how we should behave in light of the truth that wisdom is exhibited in living, we find that the answer is to (1) live in such a way that the seven attributes are seen in our lives and (2) avoid the three evidences of the lack of wisdom.

3. What are Applied ethics?

Having discovered the Meta-ethic and Normative ethic of this text we will move on to the Applied ethic. But, before we do so, we need to pause to hear James' good news.

Having discovered the Meta-ethic and Normative ethic of this text we will move on to the Applied ethic. But, before we do so, we need to pause to hear James' good news.

James 4:6 – But he gives us more grace. That is why Scripture says: "God opposes the proud but shows favor to the humble."

James declares to his readers that even though they often lack wisdom, God gives more grace. Verse six provides a point of decision. We are invited to answer the question, "Am I willing to do what it takes to exhibit wisdom in my living?"

If we answer "no," there is little reason to continue reading. If we answer "yes", however, the next verses provide the teaching on how to embrace wisdom. I'm going to assume an answer of "yes" from you and, therefore, ask you to continue reading.

> *James 4:7-10 – Submit yourselves, then, to God. Resist the devil, and he will flee from you. Come near to God and he will come near to you. Wash your hands, you sinners, and purify your hearts, you double-minded. Grieve, mourn and wail. Change your laughter to mourning and your joy to gloom. Humble yourselves before the Lord, and he will lift you up.*

Those words contain the Applied ethics. When we commit to the actions prescribed in those verses, we put ethics into practice. We apply them. Embracing wisdom begins with submission.

1. Submit – The Greek word is hupotassō meaning to put (set) yourself under authority. In other words, to surrender to Jesus' Lordship.

2. Resist.

3. Come near.

4. Wash – Clean your actions.

5. Purify – Clean your heart.

6. Mourn (to summarize all of verse 9 in one word). Explaining the call to mourn James Adamson wrote,

   > *"James is not bidding these frivolous people never to laugh again, but instead of pursuing joy all the time let them be abashed and give some serious thought to God"* (175).

   Think here of Psalm 51, the great cry of repentance from David.

7. Humble. After delivering those instructions, James devotes words to correcting his readers. He charges them to cease unfair judgement and foolish boasting. Then he arrives at a verse which concludes the passage for this chapter. It is a verse that impacted me greatly years ago during a time when, as an older youth/young man, I understood sin to be actions that were committed against God and others. That understanding, while true, is incomplete. I'll let James explain.

James 4:17 – If anyone, then, knows the good they ought to do and doesn't do it, it is sin for them.

We sin, as we know, in our *commission* of sin. However, we also sin in our *omission*. We sin when we do; we sin when do not do.

So, having heard the ethics of Christian living, are you ready to submit to Christ and live by His wisdom? Consider The Message version of James 4:7-10. These words will bring this chapter to a close and call out for you to decide. Will you or will you not show wisdom through your actions?

James 4:7-10 (MSG) – So let God work his will in you. Yell a loud no to the Devil and watch him make himself scarce. Say a quiet yes to God and he'll be there in no time. Quit dabbling in sin. Purify your inner life. Quit playing the field. Hit bottom, and cry your eyes out. The fun and games are over. Get serious, really serious. Get down on your knees before the Master; it's the only way you'll get on your feet.

20

"LOVE EXPRESSED"

In response to an inquiry Jesus explained that it is most important, in addition to loving the Lord our God with our all, to love our neighbors as we love ourselves. In the closing chapter of James' letter, he provides his readers with practical ways in which we can demonstrate that love.

1) Love expressed through financial integrity.

James 5:1-6 – Now listen, you rich people, weep and wail because of the misery that is coming on you. Your wealth has rotted, and moths have eaten your clothes. Your gold and silver are corroded. Their corrosion will testify against you and eat your flesh like fire. You have hoarded wealth in the last days. Look! The wages you failed to pay the workers who mowed your fields are crying out against you. The cries of the harvesters have reached the ears of the Lord Almighty. You have lived on earth in luxury and self-indulgence. You have fattened yourselves in the day of slaughter. You have condemned and murdered the innocent one, who was not opposing you.

If we were to stop reading at the end of verse one, we would, in error, reason that James was castigating all people of wealth. He certainly rebukes but not in blanket fashion; James rebukes the wealthy who are greedy and unjust. Those who...

a) Hoard: *James 5:3c – You have hoarded wealth in the last days.*

b) Withhold: *James 5:4 – Look! The wages you failed to pay the workers who mowed your fields are crying out against you. The cries of the harvesters have reached the ears of the Lord Almighty.*

c) Feast gluttonously: *James 5:5 – You have lived on earth in luxury and self-indulgence. You have fattened yourselves in the day of slaughter.*

Do you own a large home? Use it in hospitable ways.
Do you possess many "toys" like a boat, jet ski, 4-wheeler, or snow machine? Invite others to "play" and build community.
Do you eat well? Feed the hungry.
Do you own a company? Pay your employees well.
Do you have more than you need to the point of excess? Give some things away.

2) Love expressed through patience.

James 5:7-11 – Be patient, then, brothers and sisters, until the Lord's coming. See how the farmer waits for the land to yield its valuable crop, patiently waiting for the autumn and spring rains. You too, be patient and stand firm, because the Lord's coming is near. Don't grumble against one another, brothers and sisters, or you will be judged. The Judge is standing at the door!

Brothers and sisters, as an example of patience in the face of suffering, take the prophets who spoke in the name of the Lord. As you know, we count as blessed those who have persevered. You have heard of Job's perseverance and have seen what the Lord finally brought about. The Lord is full of compassion and mercy.

Two of the truths found in Scripture in relation to patience are that (1) the New Testament Christian thought Jesus would return within their lifetimes and (2) God's "soon" and our "soon" do not align. We would all agree that two thousand years is a lengthy amount of time to wait for the Second Coming. Really, however, think about it, you have not waited 2000 years. You have waited only since the time you became aware of the truth that He is going to return.

No matter the length of our wait, James says we are to wait in patience. What does waiting in patience look like?

a) Maintaining peace of mind.

b) Growing in knowledge and faith.

c) Committing to healthy relationships. ("Don't grumble.")

d) Remembering the suffering of others. (Job)

e) Recalling the Lord's compassion and mercy.

Gordon Poteat wrote:

[Christians] are under the grave temptation to grow halfhearted in their devotion to their Master, to surrender their hope of the kingdom of God, to lay down their weapons without having won the victory for righteousness. (67).

3) Love expressed through honesty.

James 5:12 – Above all, my brothers and sisters, do not swear— not by heaven or by earth or by anything else. All you need to say is a simple "Yes" or "No." Otherwise you will be condemned.

Here, James nearly quotes his brother Jesus. In His Sermon on the Mount, the Lord said nearly the same words. In the land of pinky swears, "so help me Gods," signed agreements, and prenuptials, we struggle to imagine a "Yes" or "No" sufficing. Keep in mind James addresses his words to Christians within a church. Therefore, his charge here is not to government officials or courts of law. Nevertheless, the principle stands. You and I should be people of our word. James Adamson writes, *"swearing is necessary only in a society where the truth is not reverenced"* (195).

Do you have an exam this week?

Don't cheat.

Did you tell your boss you would complete the assignment by Friday?

Complete it by Friday.

Did you tell your daughter you would take her to get frozen yogurt?

Get your car keys and wallet.

Did you tell your spouse you would fix the squeaky door?

Fix it.

Did you tell God you would start reading your Bible?

Read your Bible.

4) Love expressed through prayer and worship.

James 5:13-18 – Is anyone among you in trouble? Let them pray. Is anyone happy? Let them sing songs of praise. Is anyone among you sick? Let them call the elders of the church to pray over them and anoint them with oil in the name of the Lord. And the prayer offered in faith will make the sick person well; the Lord will raise them up. If they have sinned, they will be forgiven. Therefore confess your sins to each other and pray for each other so that you may be healed. The prayer of a righteous person is powerful and effective.

Elijah was a human being, even as we are. He prayed earnestly that it would not rain, and it did not rain on the land for three and a half years. Again he prayed, and the heavens gave rain, and the earth produced its crops.

What is your first response in the face of trouble? James tells us that our response should be to pray.

When you are happy and you know it, do you clap your hands and sing? That, agrees James, is a good idea.

What about when you are sick? We should be grateful for and seek help from medical professionals. We should take medication when necessary. We should seek counseling when the pain and/or confusion call for that.

And, above all, we should pray. We should pray alone; we should pray together; we should pray over each other.

Prayer is not designed as a last response. I am grateful for First Responders. I am also grateful for those of you who are the First Responders of Prayer.

Look again to the text to notice a possible connection that results in sickness.

James 5:15 – And the prayer offered in faith will make the sick person well; the Lord will raise them up. If they have sinned, they will be forgiven.

Not all sickness is the result of sin; notice the words "If they have sinned." That said, however, some sickness arises out of sin. Sin such as...

- worry

- gluttony

- rage

- unbiblical sexuality

- laziness

- lack of self-control

When you see sickness in your life caused by your sin, come clean, ask for prayer, and watch what God does. When you think that there may be a prayer request just too extreme, remember the prayer of Elijah.

> *James 5:17-18 – Elijah was a human being, even as we are. He prayed earnestly that it would not rain, and it did not rain on the land for three and a half years. Again he prayed, and the heavens gave rain, and the earth produced its crops.*

5) Love expressed through restoration.

> *James 5:19-20 – My brothers and sisters, if one of you should wander from the truth and someone should bring that person back, remember this: Whoever turns a sinner from the error of their way will save them from death and cover over a multitude of sins.*

Listen for a common theme in these words from three of Paul's letters.

> *Galatians 6:10 – Therefore, as we have opportunity, let us do good to all people, especially to those who belong to the family of believers.*

> *Ephesians 2:19 – Consequently, you are no longer foreigners and strangers, but fellow citizens with God's people and also members of his household.*

1 Timothy 5:1-2 – Do not rebuke an older man harshly, but exhort him as if he were your father. Treat younger men as brothers, older women as mothers, and younger women as sisters, with absolute purity.

Common theme? Family.

Christians are family. What do healthy families do? They take care of each other.

One aspect of caring for a family member (nuclear and church alike) is correcting one another in love. We should love one another in such a way that we make every effort to restore those who "wander from the truth." For many of us, that type of action is difficult. We are afraid of coming across as being judgmental and being called such. Whether that is the perception or not, the benefits outweigh the difficulties.

James 5:20 – Remember this: Whoever turns a sinner from the error of their way will save them from death and cover over a multitude of sins.

When we go after the one who strays, we can...

1. Save them from death (physical perhaps – as in addiction; spiritual perhaps – as in apathy)

2. Cover over sins, a multitude of them.

One person's sins harm another person. When we restore a wandering one, we save them from committing sins that could have harmed themselves and others.

- Do you notice your married friend's eyes wandering to other women? Point it out.

- Does your friend enjoy spreading gossip? Ask her not to.

- Are you aware of your friend falling back into addiction? Address it.

- Did you see inappropriate content on a friend's screen? Ask about it.

Jesus and His brother challenge us to love one another. We are now aware of several ways to accept that challenge. Let us go out and live a love that is expressed.

21

"TOO MUCH TIGGER"

One of the particularly lovable characters from A. A. Milne's Hundred Acre Wood bouncingly declares, "Bouncing is what Tiggers do best." In addition to bouncing, Tigger chooses to live a life with joy as its focus. Do you know a person who lives like Tigger? Are you that person? The "Tiggers" in life spread joy as they bounce around with positivity. That is a good thing. That is, until it is not a good thing.

Ecclesiastes 3:1-8 – There is a time for everything, and a season
for every activity under the heavens:
a time to be born and a time to die,
a time to plant and a time to uproot,
a time to kill and a time to heal,
a time to tear down and a time to build,
a time to weep and a time to laugh,
a time to mourn and a time to dance,
a time to scatter stones and a time to gather them,
a time to embrace and a time to refrain from embracing,
a time to search and a time to give up,
a time to keep and a time to throw away,
a time to tear and a time to mend,
a time to be silent and a time to speak,
a time to love and a time to hate,
a time for war and a time for peace.

Laughing and dancing belong in the life of the believer, so do weeping and mourning.

Like all leaders, Hezekiah, the thirteenth king of Judah, made wise decisions as well as foolish ones. As an example of the former, Hezekiah, when he learned of the Assyrian plan to invade Judah, wisely chose to pray. This was his prayer.

Isaiah 37:16-20 – "LORD Almighty, the God of Israel, enthroned between the cherubim, you alone are God over all the kingdoms of the earth. You have made heaven and earth. Give ear, LORD, and hear; open your eyes, LORD, and see; listen to all the words Sennacherib has sent to ridicule the living God.

"It is true, LORD, that the Assyrian kings have laid waste all these peoples and their lands. They have thrown their gods into the fire and destroyed them, for they were not gods but only wood and stone, fashioned by human hands. Now, LORD our God, deliver us from his hand, so that all the kingdoms of the earth may know that you, LORD, are the only God."

Isaiah, God's prophet to Judah, assured the king that he chose wisely.

Isaiah 37:21-22 – Then Isaiah son of Amoz sent a message to Hezekiah: "This is what the LORD, the God of Israel, says: Because you have prayed to me concerning Sennacherib king of Assyria, this is the word the LORD has spoken against him:

"Virgin Daughter Zion despises and mocks you. Daughter Jerusalem tosses her head as you flee.

Isaiah 37:33-35 – "Therefore this is what the LORD says concerning the king of Assyria: "He will not enter this city or shoot an arrow here. He will not come before it with shield or build a siege ramp against it. By the way that he came he will return; he will not enter this city," declares the LORD. "I will defend this city and save it, for my sake and for the sake of David my servant!"

As an example of a foolish decision, Hezekiah threw caution to the wind and showed (assumably with pride) Babylonian delegates all his treasure.

Isaiah 39:1-2 – At that time Marduk-Baladan son of Baladan king of Babylon sent Hezekiah letters and a gift, because he had heard of his illness and recovery. Hezekiah received the envoys gladly and showed them what was in his storehouses—the silver, the gold, the spices, the fine olive oil—his entire armory and everything found among his treasures. There was nothing in his palace or in all his kingdom that Hezekiah did not show them.

Upon learning of this folly, the Lord's prophet brings the disheartening news that, due in great part to Hezekiah's show-and-tell display, Babylon would return and take all the treasure, and the people, and the freedom from the kingdom of Judah. This, you would think, was an appropriate time to mourn. However, that is not what Hezekiah did.

Isaiah 39:8 – "The word of the LORD you have spoken is good," Hezekiah replied. For he thought, "There will be peace and security in my lifetime."

While Hezekiah did not "Tigger" the moment, he did miss the point. He missed it because of his focus on self.

Isaiah 39:8b – "There will be peace and security <u>in my lifetime</u>." (emphasis mine)

Hezekiah thought only of himself.

In this Genesis Three World people, especially people given to Tigger dispositions (As a Tigger, I would know!), can miss appropriate times to weep and mourn as they choose to see only the positive things of life. This was shamelessly portrayed in Monty Python's *Life of Brian* (a fictional next-door neighbor to Jesus). Brian, while hanging from a cross, sings …

"Always Look on the Bright Side of Life"
Songwriter: Eric Idle
Some things in life are bad
They can really make you mad
Other things just make you swear and curse
When you're chewing on life's gristle

Don't grumble, give a whistle
And this'll help things turn out for the best
And
Always look on the bright side of life
Always look on the light side of life
If life seems jolly rotten
There's something you've forgotten
And that's to laugh and smile and dance and sing
When you're feeling in the dumps
Don't be silly chumps
Just purse your lips and whistle, that's the thing
And
Always look on the bright side of life
(Come on)
Always look on the right side of life
For life is quite absurd
And death's the final word
You must always face the curtain with a bow
Forget about your sin
Give the audience a grin
Enjoy it, it's your last chance anyhow

Hezekiah chose, unwisely and selfishly, to look on the bright side. When we laugh when we should weep, we ignore reality. When we dance during times when mourning is appropriate, we miss the mark and, worse yet, mock others' grief.

What of the future of Hezekiah's children? Grandchildren? Hezekiah did not think that far ahead or, at least, chose to ignore those thoughts.

In this Genesis Three World, Christians (mostly from Western nations) often live in Hezekiah fashion. We hear of hunger in developing countries and quickly divert our attention. We concern ourselves more with keeping taxes low than addressing real needs of the impoverished. We hear of disturbing events that occur on the opposite side of town and think first not of how we can help but of how glad we are that we bought where we did. *"There will be peace and security in my lifetime."* That's too much Tigger.

22

"ENOUGH ALREADY, EEYORE!"

A less delightful character of Milne's is Eeyore who lives in Hundred Acre Wood known as "Eeyore's Gloomy Place: Rather Boggy and Sad." While Tigger causes some readers / viewers to declare "Calm down" and "Take it easy," Eeyore causes the same Hundred Acre fans to cry "Liven up" and "Why so gloomy?!" Eeyore is more tolerated than loved for who he is.

If some Christians are too Tigger-ish, others exude too much Eeyore-ism. Those Eeyore types struggle to sing, "The joy of the Lord is my strength" and "I've got that joy, joy, joy. joy down in my heart." Walter Bowie wrote …

What happens to the modern Adam excluded from the Eden of his lost innocence depends upon the attitude he adopts toward that which he cannot change. … The old story does not attempt to tell what, if anything, Adam made up his mind to do, but the whole Bible makes this plain: all that is best in the history of the human race has come from those who did not surrender to defeat but went ahead to try to correct disastrous beginnings and to put something better together out of the pieces of broken hopes and plans. Yet not by themselves! For far above what men can do is what God does in and for them. The Adam in every man that may be standing outside the Eden which his sin has forfeited can learn that there is a Second Adam through whose new nature his past can be redeemed. (515-516)

Just as there is a time to weep and mourn, there are times to dance and laugh.

Returning to the book of Genesis, we read of Adam's actions following the death of Abel, his second son, and the banishment of Cain, his eldest.

<u>Genesis 4:25</u> – Adam made love to his wife again, and she gave birth to a son and named him Seth, saying, "God has granted me another child in place of Abel, since Cain killed him."

Not that love-making is the only way to dance and laugh, but it is one way. And so is the result of new life. Seth bore the name meaning "granted." Adam and Eve, while still mourning the loss of two sons, rejoiced in God's gift (granting) of a third. A time to laugh.

Moving forward into Scripture, one notices the joy in the Psalms, even in the Psalms that start with expressions of despair.

<u>Psalm 57</u>
Have mercy on me, my God, have mercy on me, for in you I take refuge. I will take refuge in the shadow of your wings until the disaster has passed.

I cry out to God Most High, to God, who vindicates me. He sends from heaven and saves me, rebuking those who hotly pursue me— God sends forth his love and his faithfulness.

I am in the midst of lions; I am forced to dwell among ravenous beasts—men whose teeth are spears and arrows, whose tongues are sharp swords.

Be exalted, O God, above the heavens; let your glory be over all the earth. They spread a net for my feet— I was bowed down in distress. They dug a pit in my path—but they have fallen into it themselves.

My heart, O God, is steadfast, my heart is steadfast; I will sing and make music. Awake, my soul! Awake, harp and lyre! I will awaken the dawn. I will praise you, Lord, among the nations; I will sing of you among the peoples.

For great is your love, reaching to the heavens; your faithfulness reaches to the skies. Be exalted, O God, above the heavens; let your glory be over all the earth.

Those who trust in God's goodness find ways to praise Him even amid boggy and sad places and/or circumstances.

Psalm 71:10-14 – For my enemies speak against me; those who wait to kill me conspire together. They say, "God has forsaken him; pursue him and seize him, for no one will rescue him."

Do not be far from me, my God; come quickly, God, to help me. May my accusers perish in shame; may those who want to harm me be covered with scorn and disgrace.

As for me, I will always have hope; I will praise you more and more.

All believers, especially Eeyore-ish Christians, need reminders to rejoice.

In the fifth century BC, Nehemiah, the governor of Jerusalem, led the campaign of rebuilding the wall of protection around the city that the Babylonians destroyed in the sixth century. At the wall's completion and the Persian-granted permission to exiled Jews to return to their beloved city, the people set out to restore what once was a glorious homeland. Nehemiah gathered the people and called up Ezra, the prophet of God, to read the Law of Moses to the descendants of those who first received it at Mount Sinai. As the Israelites listened to the Law, conviction surely set in. They were reminded of the near countless ways they had rejected God and neglected His ways. It would appear to be a fitting time to weep and mourn. Nehemiah and Ezra did not think so.

Nehemiah 8:8-10 – They read from the Book of the Law of God, making it clear and giving the meaning so that the people understood what was being read.

Then Nehemiah the governor, Ezra the priest and teacher of the Law, and the Levites who were instructing the people said to them all, "This day is holy to the LORD your God. Do not mourn or weep." For all the people had been weeping as they listened to the words of the Law.

Nehemiah said, "Go and enjoy choice food and sweet drinks, and send some to those who have nothing prepared. This day is holy to our LORD. Do not grieve, for the joy of the LORD is your strength."

The Levitical priests echoed the charge.

Nehemiah 8:11 – The Levites calmed all the people, saying, "Be still, for this is a holy day. Do not grieve."

The people responded to the affirmative.

Nehemiah 8:12 – Then all the people went away to eat and drink, to send portions of food and to celebrate with great joy, because they now understood the words that had been made known to them.

Nehemiah, Ezra, and the Levites called for Tiggers, not Eeyores. In this Genesis Three World, there remain events worthy of parties.

23

"BEAUTY WITHIN THE BROKENESS"

As Americans revere the Bald Eagle, the people of Trinidad and Tobago revere the Scarlet Ibis. After some brief research, I can report the Caribbean Island bird is in the Threskiornithidae family of the order Pelecaniformes. All I could tell you about them when I first saw them was that they are beautiful, and they bring me joy.

During a particularly difficult time of ministry, God added to the affirmation I received from Him, loving family, and caring friends, the simple joy of seeing the beauty of a bird He crafted.

> *Genesis 1:20-23 – And God said, "Let the water teem with living creatures, and let birds fly above the earth across the vault of the sky." So God created the great creatures of the sea and every living thing with which the water teems and that moves about in it, according to their kinds, and every winged bird according to its kind. And God saw that it was good. God blessed them and said, "Be fruitful and increase in number and fill the water in the seas, and let the birds increase on the earth." And there was evening, and there was morning—the fifth day.*

As was my Monday tradition, I loaded the car with snacks, two of our three children (the oldest was in school), a stroller, and headed to our local zoo. There, my sons and I would mimic monkeys, pet goats, point at fish, extend our necks by the giraffes and arms by the elephants. One day as we made our way up the slight incline to the left of the entry, a red movement caught my eye – the movement of one of the exhibited Scarlet Ibises. It was not the first time I saw the birds but the first time I *saw* them. God struck me with their beauty. Their radiant scarlet wings reflecting the sun's rays melted me. I knew that on Tuesday, disgruntled I-want-it-my-way church members would call or stop by to "chat." I knew that my stress levels remained elevated. Yet. Yet – in that moment – I saw beauty within the brokenness.

> *Matthew 6:26 – Look at the birds of the air; they do not sow or reap or store away in barns, and yet your heavenly Father feeds them. Are you not much more valuable than they?*

As I looked at that bird of the air (albeit caged), I knew that God loved me and out of that love, He would care for and protect me. Wanting to remember that moment (not that I would have forgotten), I stepped across the "Do Not Cross" sign and helped myself to two scarlet feathers that the Ibis was no longer wearing. Over a decade and a half later, one of those feathers resides in my bathroom medicine cabinet and the other, scarlet as ever, is displayed behind glass on one of my office bookshelves.

That day at the zoo was an Elijah-moment for me. Elijah, the prophet, experienced some particularly dark ministry days. On those days he felt despair as all appeared to be for naught. Wicked Jezebel was on his heels and somberness filled his heart.

> *1 Kings 19:3-4 – Elijah was afraid and ran for his life. When he came to Beersheba in Judah, he left his servant there, while he himself went a day's journey into the wilderness. He came to a broom bush, sat down under it and prayed that he might die. "I have had enough, LORD," he said. "Take my life; I am no better than my ancestors."*

Hearing Elijah's call of despair, God provided rest and food for the prophet and then listened to him again.

> *1 Kings 19:10 – He replied, "I have been very zealous for the LORD God Almighty. The Israelites have rejected your covenant, torn down your altars, and put your prophets to death with the sword. I am the only one left, and now they are trying to kill me too."*

After that reply, Elijah experienced his Scarlet-Ibis moment.

1 Kings 19:11-13a – The LORD said, "Go out and stand on the mountain in the presence of the LORD, for the LORD is about to pass by." Then a great and powerful wind tore the mountains apart and shattered the rocks before the LORD, but the LORD was not in the wind. After the wind there was an earthquake, but the LORD was not in the earthquake. After the earthquake came a fire, but the LORD was not in the fire. And after the fire came a gentle whisper. When Elijah heard it, he pulled his cloak over his face and went out and stood at the mouth of the cave.

Elijah heard the gentle whisper; I saw the beauty of the Scarlet Ibis.

To live well in this Genesis Three World, one needs to visit caves, walk zoos, hike mountains, gaze at stars, listen to children's laughter, smell flowers in bloom, watch moose, stare as birds soar, listen to music, hold hands, and soak up the sun.

Psalm 19:1 – The heavens declare the glory of God; the skies proclaim the work of his hands.

Psalm 104
Praise the LORD, my soul. LORD my God, you are very great; you are clothed with splendor and majesty. The LORD wraps himself in light as with a garment; he stretches out the heavens like a tent and lays the beams of his upper chambers on their waters.

He makes the clouds his chariot and rides on the wings of the wind. He makes winds his messengers, flames of fire his servants. He set the earth on its foundations; it can never be moved.

You covered it with the watery depths as with a garment; the waters stood above the mountains. But at your rebuke the waters fled, at the sound of your thunder they took to flight; they flowed over the mountains, they went down into the valleys, to the place you assigned for them.

You set a boundary they cannot cross; never again will they cover the earth. He makes springs pour water into the ravines; it flows between the mountains. They give water to all the beasts of the field; the wild donkeys quench their thirst. The birds of the sky nest by the waters; they sing among the branches.

He waters the mountains from his upper chambers; the land is satisfied by the fruit of his work. He makes grass grow for the cattle, and plants for people to cultivate— bringing forth food from the earth: wine that gladdens human hearts, oil to make their faces shine, and bread that sustains their hearts.

The trees of the LORD are well watered, the cedars of Lebanon that he planted. There the birds make their nests; the stork has its home in the junipers.

The high mountains belong to the wild goats; the crags are a refuge for the hyrax. He made the moon to mark the seasons, and the sun knows when to go down. You bring darkness, it becomes night, and all the beasts of the forest prowl.

The lions roar for their prey and seek their food from God. The sun rises, and they steal away; they return and lie down in their dens. Then people go out to their work, to their labor until evening. How many are your works, LORD!

In wisdom you made them all; the earth is full of your creatures. There is the sea, vast and spacious, teeming with creatures beyond number— living things both large and small.

There the ships go to and fro, and Leviathan, which you formed to frolic there. All creatures look to you to give them their food at the proper time.

When you give it to them, they gather it up; when you open your hand, they are satisfied with good things.

When you hide your face, they are terrified; when you take away their breath, they die and return to the dust.When you send your Spirit, they are created, and you renew the face of the ground. May the glory of the LORD endure forever; may the LORD rejoice in his works—he who looks at the earth, and it trembles, who touches the mountains, and they smoke.

I will sing to the LORD all my life; I will sing praise to my God as long as I live.May my meditation be pleasing to him, as I rejoice in the LORD.

But may sinners vanish from the earth and the wicked be no more. Praise the LORD, my soul. Praise the LORD.

The psalmist's hand kept guiding his pen across the parchment as the images of God's creative glory filled his mind. One need not live in despair in brokenness. God sustains beauty even in its brokenness.

Christian theology rejects pantheism. God is *not* in all things of creation. However, God is behind all things in creation and His beauty is displayed in their beauty. Eugene Peterson stated it well when he said …

The phrase "worship the LORD in the beauty of holiness" is embedded in the experience of a wild, crashing thunderstorm. The storm is then turned into an extended metaphor in which the thunder is the voice of the Lord, qol-Yahweh. Seven great thunderclaps, seven times the voice of the Lord peals out:
*   The voice of the LORD is over the waters;*
*   the God of glory thunders,*
*   the LORD, over many waters. (verse 3 [Psalm 29], ESV)*
In the Hebrew imagination, the waters were chaos, the uncontrollable and uncontrolled, the home of Leviathan, anticreation. But when the voice of the Lord thunders over the waters, chaos becomes subject to creation: life, an illusion to

Genesis 1, our first glimpse of the beauty of holiness. Storms are splendid, beautiful, awesome. God is on display performing the beauty of holiness, and we have a ringside seat. (81)

Imagine oak trees whirling like partners in a fast-paced folk dance, the voice of the Lord calling out the moves, leaves swirling from the trees like skirts and scarves of dancers, the rhythms and movements and exchanges beautiful in holiness. (82-83)

Peterson's words skillfully express the opportunities for viewing the beauty within God's creation. They do more as well. They remind us that God's beauty is seen in more than the sights, sounds, and tastes of this world; it is seen in His holiness as well as in holy lives lived by the saints of old and the run-of-the-mill believers today.

<u>Hebrews 12:1-2</u> – Therefore, since we are surrounded by such a great cloud of witnesses, let us throw off everything that hinders and the sin that so easily entangles. And let us run with perseverance the race marked out for us, fixing our eyes on Jesus, the pioneer and perfecter of faith. For the joy set before him he endured the cross, scorning its shame, and sat down at the right hand of the throne of God.

<u>Romans 12:1</u> (MSG) – So here's what I want you to do, God helping you: Take your everyday, ordinary life—your sleeping, eating, going-to-work, and walking-around life—and place it before God as an offering.

<u>Beauty in Holiness</u>

- How beautiful it is when a new believer declares, "Jesus is Lord" and receives baptism as her church applauds.

- How beautiful it is when young love is expressed with held hands and nothing more.

- How beautiful is the forgiveness given to a friend.

- How beautiful it is when the other cheek is turned.

- How beautiful it is when the words "I apologize" are voiced (and meant).

- How beautiful it is when the rich help the poor.

- How beautiful are the feet of those who bring good news.

- How beautiful it is when deacons feed widows.

- How beautiful it is when believers open their homes to orphans.

- How beautiful it is when the young honor their elders.

- How beautiful it is when the elders encourage and equip the young.

Philippians 2:1-4 – Therefore if you have any encouragement from being united with Christ, if any comfort from his love, if any common sharing in the Spirit, if any tenderness and compassion, then make my joy complete by being like-minded, having the same love, being one in spirit and of one mind. Do nothing out of selfish ambition or vain conceit. Rather, in humility value others above yourselves, not looking to your own interests but each of you to the interests of the others.

1 Peter 1:13-16 – Therefore, with minds that are alert and fully sober, set your hope on the grace to be brought to you when Jesus Christ is revealed at his coming. As obedient children, do not conform to the evil desires you had when you lived in ignorance. But just as he who called you is holy, so be holy in all you do; for it is written: "Be holy, because I am holy."

Hope, the traveling companion of the protagonist from *The Pilgrim's Progress*, declared to Christian …

"Finally, it made me love the pursuit of holiness and long to do something for the honor and glory of the name of the Lord Jesus!" *(198-199)*

24

"SEEKING TRUE LIFE"

At Rabbit Creek Church where I serve as Senior Pastor, we have adopted the practice of three-year themes. For three years, a verse (or verses) from the Bible serves as our overarching theme. For 2022 – 2024, we chose the words of Jesus found in Matthew 10:39.

Matthew 10:39 (NLT) – If you cling to your life, you will lose it; but if you give up your life for me, you will find it.

Jesus' call upon our lives is about giving up control and about answering the call to relationship with Jesus and service to God. A well-known passage of Scripture also found in the New Testament book of Matthew provides understanding of that call.

Matthew 4:18-22 – As Jesus was walking beside the Sea of Galilee, he saw two brothers, Simon called Peter and his brother Andrew. They were casting a net into the lake, for they were fishermen. "Come, follow me," Jesus said, "and I will send you out to fish for people." At once they left their nets and followed him.

Going on from there, he saw two other brothers, James son of Zebedee and his brother John. They were in a boat with their father Zebedee, preparing their nets. Jesus called them, and immediately they left the boat and their father and followed him.

When we read this account, we observe three pivotal actions: (1) Jesus invited. (2) Those invited responded by letting go of their "known." (3) Those who let go followed Jesus into the "unknown."

1. Jesus invited.

Jesus arrived on the scene of the fishing-brother duos and issued a call, extended an invitation. "Come, follow me" Jesus said. Theologians hold varying views on the breadth of God's call. Some hold that God calls only certain people while others hold that God's salvation is open to all people. All Christian theologians, though, agree on at least a few things, one of them being the conviction that God issues the invitation. To state it another way, no one comes to God without first receiving a call to do so. Those various views, as well as the shared view, apply to the Christian understanding of the call to salvation, also known as the General Call.

Another type of call is the Specific Call. While the General Call refers to salvation, the Specific Call refers to service. The calls in Matthew 4 are calls to service. Such calls to service Jesus issued to all Christians. Notice that last word, "Christians." If, today, you are not a Christian, read this carefully – God issues a General Call to you. So, before I continue by focusing on the Specific Call, I pause here to urge you to answer the General Call.

> *John 3:16 – For God so loved the world that he gave his one and only Son, that whoever believes in him shall not perish but have eternal life.*

> *John 14:6 – Jesus answered, "I am the way and the truth and the life. No one comes to the Father except through me."*

Returning to the topic of Specific Call, we recall that it is a call to service. For Peter, Andrew, James, and John, that call was to serve as four of the twelve closest disciples of Jesus.

2. Those invited responded by letting go of their "known."

The "known" for the two sets of brothers included nets and boats; it also included family, long-embraced routines, familiar territory, job security, beds in which they slept within houses they called home, and many other mental and muscle-memory activities. Jesus, when He invites, calls people out of the known. For us that can be,

- routines

- jobs

- homes

- schedules

- long-held traditions

- long-adopted habits

3. <u>Those who let go, followed Jesus into the "unknown."</u>

Jesus' invitation reminds me of the foundational story of Abram. As Genesis chapter eleven draws to a close, so does the author's focus on the world-in-general. As chapter twelves begins, the scope of the biblical narrative narrows to a people that God formed and chose through which His salvation plan would arrive. It began with a call to a man named Abram, a call to leave his "known" and walk into an unknown location and life.

Genesis 12:1-3 – The LORD had said to Abram, "Go from your country, your people and your father's household to the land I will show you. "I will make you into a great nation, and I will bless you; I will make your name great, and you will be a blessing. I will bless those who bless you, and whoever curses you I will curse; and all peoples on earth will be blessed through you."

"To a land I will show you" is all the description and map that Abram received. The four fishermen of Matthew received even less.

Matthew 4:19 – "Come, follow me," Jesus said, "and I will send you out to fish for people."

Upon the basis of that very limited in detail call, the brothers followed Jesus into the unknown.

Is it any wonder that conversations like the following occurred later?

Matthew 8:19-20 – Then a teacher of the law came to him and said, "Teacher, I will follow you wherever you go." Jesus replied,

"Foxes have dens and birds have nests, but the Son of Man has no place to lay his head."

John 14:5-6 – Thomas said to him, "Lord, we don't know where you are going, so how can we know the way?" Jesus answered, "I am the way and the truth and the life. No one comes to the Father except through me.

I'm inviting you to answer your invitation from Jesus to follow Him. Hearing my (and, more importantly, His) invitation, you may be asking how He's calling you and/or questioning if He is giving you a Specific Call at all. If so, listen to His words as found in John 14.

John 14:15 – "If you love me, keep my commands."

And John 15.

John 15:8-9 – "This is to my Father's glory, that you bear much fruit, showing yourselves to be my disciples. As the Father has loved me, so have I loved you. Now remain in my love."

With those verses in mind, I wrote a prayer that I encourage you to pray along with me.

Father, thank you for your call to salvation. Thank you also for your call to service. Help me to answer that call. Show me what you want me to do for you and for others. Guide my steps. Show me what changes I need to make. Help me to willingly and cheerfully make those changes through the power of your Spirit.

Show me how you have gifted me and how I can use those gifts to glorify you and help others.

"Search me, God, and know my heart; test me and know my anxious thoughts. See if there is any offensive way in me, and lead me in the way everlasting" (Psalm 139:23-24).

In the name of Jesus I pray. Amen.

25

"NOTHING, REALLY"

Praise be to God and thanks be to my parents for the fact that I grew up in a home where I never asked the questions,

"Am I loved?"

"Will my parents abandon me?"

Praise be to God and thanks be to Vonda Kay for the fact that I am in a marriage where I never ask the questions,

"Am I loved?"

"Will my wife leave me?"

The unquestioned knowledge of the love and support of my wife today, as too from my parents in my childhood home, provides among other things a great sense of security. The fact that my mind is free from having to wonder if I am loved allows my thoughts to focus on other things, the most important of which is how I can live my everyday, ordinary life for God.

As with my parents and my wife, my God provides a relationship where I am secure and free from any worry that He will cease to love and/or care for me. My parents and my wife love and support me exceptionally well. God loves and supports me perfectly.

I ask you today, do you have such security? Do you know that you know that you know that God loves you and will not abandon you?

Recently the church I serve embraced a theme for this year entitled "Find Your Life." It is primarily about discovering specific ways and opportunities through which we can serve God. The Bible tells us that we are the salt of the world. We are not worth our salt when, while attempting to serve God, doubts regarding God's love and our security float around our brains, if not fill our heads. When we know that we are secure, we can focus on finding our place of ministry.

I direct your attention, therefore, to the primary passage of Scripture, which, when believed, provides a freeing sense of security grounded in God's truth. The passage is Romans 8:31-39. Before we read that text, allow me to provide some context. The first thirty verses of Romans, chapter eight, beautifully set the stage for verses 31-39.

Verses one through four assure us that for those who trust Christ Jesus there is no condemnation.

> *Romans 8:1 – Therefore, there is now no condemnation for those who are in Christ Jesus.*

Within verses five through seventeen (and later in verses twenty through twenty-seven), we become aware of the life and guidance provided to believers through the Spirit.

> *Romans 8:11 – And if the Spirit of him who raised Jesus from the dead is living in you, he who raised Christ from the dead will also give life to your mortal bodies because of his Spirit who lives in you.*

Verses eighteen through twenty-one assure us of the coming glory of Romans 8:18-19.

> *Romans 8:18-19 – I consider that our present sufferings are not worth comparing with the glory that will be revealed in us. For the creation waits in eager expectation for the children of God to be revealed.*

Verse twenty-eight provides encouragement even within chaos.

> *Romans 8:28 – And we know that in all things God works for the good of those who love him, who have been called according to his purpose.*

(Special note: God does not cause all things. Therefore, most of the painful experiences in life aren't the work of God. However, God is not thwarted by them.) Gerald Cragg stated it well when he wrote:

There is no sentimental attempt to persuade ourselves that evil things are actually good. They remain what they are; but though bad in themselves, they have lost the power to defeat us. (524).

Verses twenty-nine and thirty assure us of God's love working through His sovereignty. Within these verses we read about the truth that God has foreknowledge and therefore from that knowledge flows predestination, justification and glorification.

Romans 8:29-30 – For those God foreknew he also predestined to be conformed to the image of his Son, that he might be the firstborn among many brothers and sisters. And those he predestined, he also called; those he called, he also justified; those he justified, he also glorified.

I appreciate Herbert Lockyer's explanation of the teaching of predestination.

What must be borne in mind is the fact that predestination is not God's predetermining from past ages who should and who should not be saved. Scripture does not teach this view. What it does teach is that this doctrine of predestination concerns the future of believers. Predestination is the divine determining the glorious consummation of all who through faith, and surrender become the Lord's. He has determined beforehand that each child of his will reach adoption, or "the son-placing" at his resurrection when Christ returns. It has been determined beforehand that all who are truly Christ's be conformed to His image. (153)

With those five contextual notes in hand, we will now proceed to our primary text of Scripture.

Romans 8:31-39 – What, then, shall we say in response to these things? If God is for us, who can be against us? He who did not spare his own Son, but gave him up for us all—how will he not also, along with him, graciously give us all things? Who will bring any charge against those whom God has chosen? It is God who justifies. Who then is the one who condemns? No one. Christ Jesus who died—more than that, who was raised to life—is at the right hand of God and is also interceding for us. Who shall separate us from the love of Christ? Shall trouble or hardship or persecution or famine or nakedness or danger or sword? As it is written: "For your sake we face death all day long; we are considered as sheep to be slaughtered."

No, in all these things we are more than conquerors through him who loved us. For I am convinced that neither death nor life, neither angels nor demons, neither the present nor the future, nor any powers, neither height nor depth, nor anything else in all creation, will be able to separate us from the love of God that is in Christ Jesus our Lord.

Note the format of the first three verses. Matthew Black, in his commentary on the text, highlights that Paul followed the "law-suit pattern" as found often in the Old Testament. The "law-suit pattern" here in Romans 8 is seen in the barrage of questions (125-26).

Imagine a doubtful believer on the stand facing the bombardment of inquiries!

As we study these questions, we find profound assurances in regard to the security of believers. Those assurances arise out of some key biblical truths within the passage. Look to those key biblical truths with me.

<u>Key Biblical Truths</u>

<u>Romans 8:32</u> – He who did not spare his own Son, but gave him up for us all—how will he not also, along with him, graciously give us all things?

1) God gave His Son and He continues to give, to provide.

Romans 8:33b – It is God who justifies.

2) It is God who justifies.

Those whom God has chosen are justified. Justification is the act of taking "account of the seriousness of our wrongdoing, but our whole life is taken up into a new relationship with God" (Knox). Richard Hays defines justification as "the event whereby persons are set or declared to be in right relationship to God" (3:1129). It is important to notice the word "in" in this definition. The believer does not mysteriously become right; he is said to be so by God."

Romans 8:34c – Christ Jesus who died—more than that, who was raised to life—is at the right hand of God and is also interceding for us.

3) Jesus is with the Father interceding (advocating) for us.

Paul intersperses those truths among the barrage of questions. Then he brings the gavel down and proclaims the verdict.

Romans 8:37-39 – No, in all these things we are more than conquerors through him who loved us. For I am convinced that neither death nor life, neither angels nor demons, neither the present nor the future, nor any powers, neither height nor depth, nor anything else in all creation, will be able to separate us from the love of God that is in Christ Jesus our Lord.

In the assuring words of Herbert Lockyer, *"God's perfect salvation covers the past, includes the present and embraces the future..." (161).*

Today, if you are a Christian and yet still wonder if your salvation is secure, I find myself wanting to simply say to you "Stop it!" But I realize that will not do. You most likely have reason for your doubt. Past pain. Current struggle. History of being abandoned and/or let down. Etc. Nevertheless, listen. God is not your neglectful parent or betraying spouse. God is not a seasonal friend. God didn't design the pain you are now in. Satan, not God, came to steal, kill, and destroy. Believe those truths. Hold to those truths. Read that passage again and within those words find your security.

Romans 8:37-39 — *No, in all these things we are more than conquerors through him who loved us. For I am convinced that neither death nor life, neither angels nor demons, neither the present nor the future, nor any powers, neither height nor depth, nor anything else in all creation, will be able to separate us from the love of God that is in Christ Jesus our Lord.*

26

"WHAT OF HOLINESS?"

<u>*1 Peter 1:16*</u> *says, "Be holy, because I am holy."*

Those words must have startled Peter's readers just as they had done to the hearers of Leviticus twenty centuries before them.

"Be holy, because I am holy."

Those are the words of God. Consider the magnitude of that charge, given that it came from the mouth of God. Only the most ignorant person would argue against God's holiness. Certainly, God is holy. That makes sense. Holy means set apart and different. The Creator of the heavens and the earth certainly qualifies for that description. God's holiness seems obvious.

But what of our holiness? Is such a thing even possible? If so, how in the world can we, people with self-seeking hearts who gossip, covet, lust, speak unkind words, lose our tempers, judge unfairly and rebel, achieve holiness?

With similar thoughts in mind, Herbert Lockyer wrote, "Weeds grow of themselves; flowers are planted" (218). Lockyer points us to the truth that we will achieve only weed-worthy holiness on our own, under the power of our strength and determination.

However, another option avails itself. If we are wise, we choose that other option.

<u>*2 Thessalonians 2:13-17*</u> *– But we ought always to thank God for you, brothers and sisters loved by the Lord, because God chose you as first fruits to be saved through the sanctifying work of the Spirit and through belief in the truth. He called you to this through*

our gospel, that you might share in the glory of our Lord Jesus Christ.

So then, brothers and sisters, stand firm and hold fast to the teachings we passed on to you, whether by word of mouth or by letter. May our Lord Jesus Christ himself and God our Father, who loved us and by his grace gave us eternal encouragement and good hope, encourage your hearts and strengthen you in every good deed and word.

Prior to these verses, Paul explained the dreadful future awaiting those people who surrendered to wickedness rather than to God.

2 Thessalonians 2:10b – They perish because they refused to love the truth and so be saved.

Indicating a transition to a happier note, Paul chose to establish the contrasts as we saw in our passage. Read the first two verses again.

2 Thessalonians 2:13-14 – But we ought always to thank God for you, brothers and sisters loved by the Lord, because God chose you as first fruits to be saved through the sanctifying work of the Spirit and through belief in the truth. He called you to this through our gospel, that you might share in the glory of our Lord Jesus Christ.

"But we ought always to thank God for you." For Paul's recipients the future was not dreadful. Neither was to be the present. They could find encouragement in the knowledge of the fact that,

1. God chose them.

2. The Spirit was with them (and working in them).

3. They had access to the truth.

4. They would share in the glory of the Lord Jesus Christ.

As we look to his whole text, we do well to ask a few questions and then to seek the answers:

Question #1: What is the sanctifying work of the Spirit?

Question #2: What is belief in the truth?

Question #3: How do we stand firm and hold fast?

Question #1: What is the sanctifying work of the Spirit?

As we answer that question, we need first to understand who may experience the sanctifying work.

> *Romans 8:9 – You, however, are not in the realm of the flesh but are in the realm of the Spirit, if indeed the Spirit of God lives in you. And if anyone does not have the Spirit of Christ, they do not belong to Christ.*

All Christians and only Christians may experience the sanctifying work. So, what is that sanctifying work? It is the work done by the Holy Spirit within the lives of Christians that transforms them more and more into the image of Christ. As the transformation takes place tangible changes can be observed.

> *Galatians 5:22-23 – But the fruit of the Spirit is love, joy, peace, forbearance, kindness, goodness, faithfulness, gentleness and self-control. Against such things there is no law.*

As you see that fruit increase in your life, you will know that the Spirit is at work. If you do not see that fruit increasing, you need to, in the words of Paul, "Keep in step with the Spirit."

Question #2: What is belief in the truth?

Jesus referred to himself as the Way, the Truth and the Life. Truth originates in and flows through Jesus. To believe in the truth is to believe in Jesus. Additionally, believing truth is about maintaining faith in His word. We are to believe in the Bible, allowing it, through the Spirit, to change us through and through. A special note to help us here. The word translated "belief" in the phrase "belief in the truth" is the Greek word Πίστις (pistis). In the New Testament, the word pistis is most often translated as "faith." That is important to note because when the Bible speaks of "belief," it is a faith that as James wrote, is dead without works/actions. So, what is belief in the truth? It is faith in God and His word expressed through action.

1 John 2:4 – Whoever says, "I know him," but does not do what He commands is a liar, and the truth is not in that person.

Question #3: How do we stand firm and hold fast?

We stand firm and hold fast by responding to the Spirit and living in light of the truth.

Reliance on the Spirit and holding to the truth enable us to stand firm and hold fast. Without one or the other, our standing will fall flat, and our hold will slip. Ignorance is not bliss. We gain knowledge through Spirit and word and, therefore, gain the motivation and strength we need to live for God.

2 Thessalonians 2:16-17 – May our Lord Jesus Christ himself and God our Father, who loved us and by his grace gave us eternal encouragement and good hope, encourage your hearts and strengthen you in every good deed and word.

How full are your encouragement and hope tanks? You can fill them by doing three things.

1. Submit to the sanctifying work of the Spirit.

2. Believe (in faith and action) in the truth.

3. Stand firm and hold fast to teachings.

27

"SERVICE TIME"

For more than 40 years, Dr. Wally Christian taught in the Religion Department of Baylor University. In addition to several other courses, Dr. Christian taught Old Testament Survey, a class in which I enrolled, as did one of my dorm roommates. At some point during the semester, after Dr. Christian returned our graded exams, my friend was less than pleased with his score – the grade was a sign of things to come. In due time, my friend's father, who was footing the tuition bill for his son, learned of the sub-par grades. Attempting to draw on his dad's mercy, my friend said, "Dad, I may not know Moses, but I do know Jesus!" He soon thereafter transferred to a different university. While his was a statement of self-defense rather than a well-informed theological treatise, it was, unbeknownst to him, a statement that, while not exactly so, came close to articulating one of Paul's arguments in his letter to the Galatians.

> *Galatians 5:1 – It is for freedom that Christ has set us free. Stand firm, then, and do not let yourselves be burdened again by a yoke of slavery.*

While our main scripture text for this chapter comes twelve verses later, we need to start here in verse one.

Historical Context: Paul, here, was writing to Christians who were receiving different messages regarding teachings on what was necessary for them to do to live as followers of Jesus. There were those who taught that to be a good Christian, you needed to follow Jewish law, with a particular focus on the continuation of religious-based circumcision. Paul urges the Galatians to refuse to submit to the slavery of religious law keeping. Those holding an opposing view were referred to as Judaizers. Scot McKnight summarizes the issue well.

The Galatian converts were insecure about their moral guidance and in particular about how to fight off the flesh. The Judaizers, having been taught that the law of Moses is God's moral guide, contended that it would enable the Galatian converts to fight off the flesh. Paul contends that the flesh has actually been put to death already and that the means of moral guidance has already been given: God's Spirit. (265)

Paul taught well. So why, even still, did many Galatian converts submit to the Judaizers' teachings? J. Barclay explains, "With no law to distinguish right from wrong, and no rituals to deal with transgressions and provide assurance, their security and self-confidence were somewhat shaky" (qtd in McKnight 264).

The comfort found in rule-keeping and religiosity attracts many.

Over the fourteen years my family and I have lived in our home, we have done much painting, exterior and interior. During one project, as the new paint, which was labeled as some shade of gray, met the wall, I could not tell that it was indeed gray. It looked white to me. Gray is much more difficult to see in comparison to identifying black and white. As with paint, so too with life. That is why many of us are attracted to a list of things to avoid and a list of okays. Checklists may work for a while, but they will not suffice through and through.

In life you face grays.

- Should I give this man cash even though I'm quite sure he is not going to use it on bus fare or food?

- Should I vote the party line even when I know that the candidate is living immorally?

- Is it okay to lie in order to bring the Good News where it is not allowed?

- To what degree should I support my family member or friend who lives outside the biblical worldview regarding life choices of sexuality and gender?

- How expensive of a vehicle should I purchase?

- If I drink responsibly, should I drink when I'm with my friend who struggles with alcohol?

- How do I balance freedom and responsibility (think Covid rules)?

- In what way should I discipline my children?

Within the fifth chapter, Paul articulates a beautifully simple yet far-reaching answer to such questions.

> *Galatians 5:6 – For in Christ Jesus neither circumcision nor uncircumcision has any value. The only thing that counts is faith expressing itself through love.*

Notice the two key ingredients. Faith and Love. Faith without love is heartless. Love without faith is spineless.

So, how do we answer life's questions? Well, hold on to that question. We will return to it after we return to the text for a further look.

> *Galatians 5:13-15 – You, my brothers and sisters, were called to be free. But do not use your freedom to indulge the flesh; rather, serve one another humbly in love. For the entire law is fulfilled in keeping this one command: "Love your neighbor as yourself." If you bite and devour each other, watch out or you will be destroyed by each other.*

Paul, in verses one through twelve, argued for their freedom. In verse thirteen, he attempts to nip in the bud any abuse of such freedom. How is the freedom in Christ to be used? In service to others.

Out of an abundance of caution, not wanting to bring images that would be too negative to the minds of their readers, many biblical translators translate the Greek words Δουλεύετε ἀλλήλοις (douleuete allelois) as "serve one another humbly." While I admire their caution, a better choice I believe, is to translate them more literally as we find in the NRSV.

> *Galatians 5:13 (NRSV) – For you were called to freedom, brothers and sisters; only do not use your freedom as an*

opportunity for self-indulgence, but through love become slaves to one another.

I like the translation of that verse, especially when we look at it through the lens of 5:1.

Galatians 5:1 (NIV) – It is for freedom that Christ has set us free. Stand firm, then, and do not let yourselves be burdened again by a yoke of slavery.

Galatians 5:13 (NRSV) – For you were called to freedom, brothers and sisters; only do not use your freedom as an opportunity for self-indulgence, but through love become slaves to one another.

While we are no longer slaves to law and rule, we are to serve each other in such a way that we recognize that we, while equals, are to serve one another humbly. I find Raymond Stamm's words from sixty years ago very helpful here.

The persistence of translators in saying servants instead of "slaves" reflects the sensitiveness of the church to the charge that Paul is fostering a slave mentality. But he is speaking of a new kind of slavery in which every man and his brother are free but willingly perform the most menial tasks for each other. Neither takes advantage of the other's voluntary self-enslavement, and each treats the other as better than himself. (Inter pg. 556)

Even for non-rule followers, rule following often proves easier than self-denial.

- Don't lie? Sure.

- Don't steal? No problem.

- Interrupt my schedule to sit and listen to a person in need? Maybe.

- Spend money to go on a mission trip rather than to a beach? Really?!

So here we are again asking questions. I promised you that we would return to the question, how do we answer life's questions? Paul tells us.

Galatians 5:16-18 – *So I say, walk by the Spirit, and you will not gratify the desires of the flesh. For the flesh desires what is contrary to the Spirit, and the Spirit what is contrary to the flesh. They are in conflict with each other, so that you are not to do whatever you want. But if you are led by the Spirit, you are not under the law.*

When we need answers to life's questions, the place to go is to the person of the Holy Spirit. That works by praying for His leadership and guidance as you read Scripture and listen for His lead.

Will we make mistakes? Yes. Will we disagree on what we think is the right choice? You bet. But we are much better off as slaves to the Spirit and to each other than we are to the law.

I am thankful for Moses. But I am so much more thankful for Jesus.

"PATH TO SATISFACTION"

Eve reached for it. Solomon strove for it. Mick Jagger and Britney Spears sang about it. We all seek it. What is it?

I speak of satisfaction. While a quick Google search will place nearly countless words of advice and techniques before you to achieve satisfaction, one verse of Scripture provides the actual path.

Luke 6:21a – Blessed are you who hunger now, for you will be satisfied.

Matthew's more well-known account of Jesus' words provide further explanation.

Matthew 5:6 – Blessed are those who hunger and thirst for righteousness, for they will be filled.

The answer to finding satisfaction, we see, therefore, is to hunger and thirst for righteousness. Let's unpack this biblical truth before we head out to find satisfaction. Read Matthew's text again.

Matthew 5:6 – Blessed are those who hunger and thirst for righteousness, for they will be filled.

Matthew 5:6 – Blessed are those who hunger and thirst for righteousness, for they will be filled [satisfied].

We begin our unpacking by observing key words within this verse.

1. Blessed – Blessed is "divine joy and perfect happiness."

2. Hunger – To hunger is to have an intense desire for filling or completeness.

3. Thirst – To thirst is to long for the necessities of life. Where there is water, there is life. Where there is no water, there is no life.

4. Righteousness – The Greek word for righteousness is derived from the root word Δίκη (deé-kay) which means justice. To hunger and thirst for righteousness is to desire and long for justice.

   Michael Wilkins writes, *"Those who hunger and thirst for righteousness desire to see justice executed on earth, they long to experience a deeper ethical righteousness in their own lives, and most of all they crave God's promised salvation come to the earth." (207)*

   Notice Wilkins' detailing of a three-fold hunger and thirst. For,

   > 1) earthly justice
   > 2) ethical behavior in our own lives
   > 3) salvation

5. Satisfaction – You will notice that while the Greek word in Luke is translated "will be filled," Matthew is translated "will be satisfied." It is the same word. The Greek word conjures up an image from grazing livestock. The word means to gorge until full. Livestock seem always to be eating. That is a good image to grasp. We, too, should always be feasting. Of gluttony I do not speak, but rather of a continual, everyday-ordinary, longing for God's righteousness. As Norval Geldenhuys wrote, "So also those who are spiritually hungry, those who realise their own unworthiness and need and who yearn for the fullness of life which He brings, will receive the blessing" (210).

Elizabeth provides a beautiful true-life example. We meet Elizabeth in the opening chapter of the Gospel of Luke.

Luke 1:5-7 – In the time of Herod king of Judea there was a priest named Zechariah, who belonged to the priestly division of Abijah; his wife Elizabeth was also a descendant of Aaron. Both of them were righteous in the sight of God, observing all the Lord's commands and decrees blamelessly. But they were childless because Elizabeth was not able to conceive, and they were both very old.

When we hear this introduction to Elizabeth, we are informed of the condition of her heart and her womb. Elizabeth's heart was devout; her womb was barren. For five decades, Elizabeth and Zechariah longed to conceive a child. For five decades, God did not fulfill their longings. Nevertheless, throughout the waiting and not seeing years, Elizabeth and her husband continued to honor, worship, and live for God.

Luke 1:6 – Both of them were righteous in the sight of God, observing all the Lord's commands and decrees blamelessly.

Their faithfulness did not rely on God consenting to their requests. They lived lives of righteousness, the Bible tells us. Therefore, we know that they:

- worshiped
- obeyed the law
- loved each other
- cared for the poor
- loved their neighbors
- gave money generously
- served willingly
- and more.

While they hoped and prayed for an answer, they worshiped, nonetheless. As they worshiped, they hungered and thirsted for righteousness. And what does God promise to those who hunger and thirst for righteousness?

Matthew 5:6 – *Blessed are those who hunger and thirst for righteousness, for they will be filled.*

The barren womb gave way to the birth of the way-maker for the coming Messiah, Jesus Christ.

Matthew 3:1-3 – *In those days John the Baptist came, preaching in the wilderness of Judea and saying, "Repent, for the kingdom of heaven has come near." This is he who was spoken of through the prophet Isaiah: "A voice of one calling in the wilderness, 'Prepare the way for the Lord, make straight paths for him.'"*

Elizabeth's story, we recognize, is unique. Not all barren wombs are filled. However, her story is not isolated. God continues to fill and satisfy women and men who seek Him and hunger and thirst for righteousness.

As we live together, we must do so as hungry and thirsty people. We must seek justice, love mercy, and walk humbly.

29

"EDEN RESTORED"

Knowledge of the resiliency of the post-fall beauty of creation and of holiness provides hope for those who search for it even while still surrounded by brokenness. Knowledge of God's continued presence does, too.

We need not expect turns and events which have nothing to do with His lordship and are not directly in some sense acts of His lordship. This Lord is never absent, passive, non-responsible or impotent, but always present active, responsible and omnipotent. He is never dead, but always living; never sleeping, but always awake; never uninterested, but always concerned; never merely waiting in any respect, but even where He seems to wait, even where He permits, always holding the initiative. In this consists His co-existence with the creature. (Barth quoted in Peterson 103-104)

With a chapter devoted mainly to a theological explanation of the assurance of salvation for Christ-followers, Paul makes room for mention of creation's restoration.

<u>Romans 8:19-22</u> – For the creation waits in eager expectation for the children of God to be revealed. For the creation was subjected to frustration, not by its own choice, but by the will of the one who subjected it, in hope that the creation itself will be liberated from its bondage to decay and brought into the freedom and glory of the children of God.

We know that the whole creation has been groaning as in the pains of childbirth right up to the present time.

Paul, taught by the Spirit, understood that while men and women would be redeemed, so would creation. Just as the children of Eve would be freed from pain, the creation of God would be freed from thorns.

Expounding on his conviction that the apostle Paul considered the coming new creation to be the restored present creation, N.T. Wright reasons that creation itself is waiting for God to restore it and it is looking forward to its proper stewards (humanity) to care for it (from a June 7, 2022, lecture at George W. Truett Seminary). This imagery and explanation harmonize with the restorative passages of John's revelation. Surely with the texts of Genesis chapters one and two in mind, John wrote …

> *<u>Revelation 21:22-22:5</u> – I did not see a temple in the city, because the Lord God Almighty and the Lamb are its temple. The city does not need the sun or the moon to shine on it, for the glory of God gives it light, and the Lamb is its lamp. The nations will walk by its light, and the kings of the earth will bring their splendor into it. On no day will its gates ever be shut, for there will be no night there. The glory and honor of the nations will be brought into it. Nothing impure will ever enter it, nor will anyone who does what is shameful or deceitful, but only those whose names are written in the Lamb's book of life.*
>
> *Then the angel showed me the river of the water of life, as clear as crystal, flowing from the throne of God and of the Lamb down the middle of the great street of the city. On each side of the river stood the tree of life, bearing twelve crops of fruit, yielding its fruit every month. And the leaves of the tree are for the healing of the nations. No longer will there be any curse. The throne of God and of the Lamb will be in the city, and his servants will serve him. They will see his face, and his name will be on their foreheads. There will be no more night. They will not need the light of a lamp or the light of the sun, for the Lord God will give them light. And they will reign for ever and ever.*

Within that text an image brings the reader right back to the pre-Genesis, pre-broken world.

<u>Revelation 22:2b</u> – On each side of the river stood the tree of life, bearing twelve crops of fruit, yielding its fruit every month. And the leaves of the tree are for the healing of the nations.

The right-side placed bookend beautifully bears the message of the left-side placed bookend.

<u>Genesis 2:15-17</u> – The LORD God took the man and put him in the Garden of Eden to work it and take care of it. And the LORD God commanded the man, "You are free to eat from any tree in the garden; but you must not eat from the tree of the knowledge of good and evil, for when you eat from it you will certainly die."

As Eden is restored, so again will access to the trees of knowledge of good and evil and life. God's banishment of the first couple was an act of mercy.

<u>Genesis 3:22</u> – And the LORD God said, "The man has now become like one of us, knowing good and evil. He must not be allowed to reach out his hand and take also from the tree of life and eat, and live forever."

When all brokenness is mended and all creation is restored, the continuation of that act of mercy will no longer be necessary. God will allow access to the tree of life. *"Taste and see that the LORD is good"* will never have been more true.

Epilogue

As you learned in the introduction to this book, I am a John 3:16 / Romans 12:1 / Jude 21 guy. As our time in this book comes to a close, I want you to reflect on <u>Jude 21</u> – *keep yourselves in God's love as you wait for the mercy of our Lord Jesus Christ to bring you to eternal life.*

While those words have been in the Bible since its canonization, I "found" them just over thirty years ago. As a Christian, I find great assurance and direction within those words of Jude, another brother of Jesus. Jude 21 assures me that God loves me and welcomes me to reside in Him and His mercy will bring me into eternal life. The same verse directs me to "keep" and to "wait". This Genesis Three World will try to hinder our "keeping" and weaken our "waiting". Consider with me how we can overcome those attempts.

As the brokenness in this world flexes its muscles and tries to weaken your "keeping," hold strongly to the assurance of Jude. Remain in God's love by never taking it for granted and by never attempting to run away from it when pride, shame, or regret call your name. Remember the tears of Jesus? No, not the ones for Lazarus. The ones for Jerusalem.

> *<u>Luke 19:41-42</u> – As he approached Jerusalem and saw the city, he wept over it and said, "If you, even you, had only known on this day what would bring you peace—but now it is hidden from your eyes."*

His words there, coupled with earlier ones spoken about how He wanted to gather the people of Jerusalem "as a chicken gathers her young ones under her wings" (<u>Matthew 23:37</u>) – if only the people of Jerusalem would welcome His love. They did not keep themselves in God's love; they rejected it.

Just as it does your "keeping", the brokenness of this Genesis Three World mounts an attack on your "waiting". Waiting is not for wimps. For good reason, a synonym for it is "long-suffering." Nevertheless, we who follow the One who "is not slow in keeping his promise, as some understand slowness" (<u>2 Peter 3:9</u>), have no other option than to wait. We wait for . . .

- Healing

- Answers

- Wisdom

- Restoration

- Comfort

- Salvation

- Heaven

We wait for God to act.

As we wait, we do well to remember all the times God has been faithful in the past as we trust that He will remain faithful - now and forever. You and I will live in this Genesis Three World for as long as God chooses to keep us here. In the meantime, live by <u>Jude 21</u> – *keep yourselves in God's love as you wait for the mercy of our Lord Jesus Christ to bring you to eternal life.*

Special Thanks To...

Mom and Dad –

You taught me the love of God. Thank you!

Kate, Max, and Sam –

You inspire me to walk the talk. I'm proud of you!

Braden –

We love the same woman – your wife and my little girl. I'm happy you are my son-in-law.

Charles and DeeAnna –

You raised an amazing daughter. Thank you.

Rabbit Creek Church –

You are an amazing family of brothers and sisters. Thank you for trusting me.

Carol Gilliland –

You are a great friend whose support and encouragement are priceless. Thank you for your patience with my Pentel habits.

Mark T. Goodman, DMin.

Works Cited

Adamson, James B. The New International Commentary on the New Testament: The Epistle of James. Grand Rapids, MI: William B. Eerdmans, 1976.

"Addiction Statistics." AddictionCenter.com, https://www.addictioncenter.com/addiction/addiction-statistics/ Accessed 4 Aug. 2022.

Archana, EC. "10 Influential People Showed The World That Humility Is All That Matters." IndiaTimes.com, https://www.indiatimes.com/trending/human-interest/world-leaders-humble-habits-simplicity-is-all-that-matters-376449.html Accessed 8 Sept 2022.

Black, Matthew. "Romans." New Century Bible. London: Marshall, Morgan, and Scott, 1973.

Bowie, Walter R. The Interpreter's Bible. Ed. George Arthur Buttrick. Vol.1. New York: Abingdon, 1952.

Bunyan, John. Revision by Alan Vermilye. The Pilgrim's Progress. Brown Chair Books, 2021.

Cadmus, Paul. "The Seven Deadly Sins: Avarice." MetMuseum.org, https://www.metmuseum.org/art/collection/search/486327#:~:text=Of%20the%20series%2C%20Cadmus%20explained,you%20all%20are%2C%20too.%22 Accessed 17 July 2022.

"Chart of Old Testament Prophecies Fulfilled by Jesus." About-Jesus.org, http://www.aboutbibleprophecy.com/ Accessed 18 July 2022.

Conyers, A.J. A Basic Christian Theology. Nashville, TN: B&H Academic. 1995.

Cragg, Gerald R. The Interpreter's Bible. Ed. George Arthur Buttrick. Vol. 9. New York: Abingdon, 1954.

Day, Beth (Elizabeth Dayton). "Three Gates [of Gold]." <u>Poetry Explorer.net</u>, https://www.poetryexplorer.net/poem.php?id=10024996 Accessed 18 April 2023.

DeYoung, Rebecca Konyndyk. "Resistance to the Demands of Love." <u>Christian Reflection – Acedia</u>. Ed. Robert B. Kruschwitz. Waco, TX: Center for Christian Ethics, 2013.

Erickson, Millard J. <u>Concise Dictionary of Christian Theology</u>. Grand Rapids, MI: Baker, 1994.

Forbis, Wesley L. <u>The Baptist Hymnal</u>. Nashville, TN: Convention Press, 1991.

Geldenhuys, Norval. <u>The Gospel of Luke - The New International Commentary on the New Testament</u>. Grand Rapids: Eerdmans, 1951.

Goodman, Mark T. <u>The Ordinary Way: A Unique Way to Live</u>. Dallas: Five Stones Press, 2019.

Hays, Richard. "Justification." Page 1129 in vol. 3 of <u>The Anchor Bible Dictionary</u>. Edited by D. N. Freedman. 6 vols. New York: Doubleday, 1992.

Idle, Eric. "Always Look on the Bright Side of Life." <u>Monty Python's Life of Brian</u>. Warner Records, 1979.

Knox, John. <u>The Interpreter's Bible.</u> Ed. George A. Buttrick. Vol. 9. New York: Abingdon, 1954.

Lederer, Richard. <u>Crazy English: The Ultimate Joy Ride Through Our Language</u>. New York: Pocket Books, 1989.

Lockyer, Herbert. <u>All the Doctrines of the Bible</u>. Grand Rapids: Zondervan, 1964.

McKnight, Scot. <u>The NIV Application Commentary</u>. Grand Rapids: Zondervan, 1995.

Murphy, Edward F. <u>The Handbook for Spiritual Warfare</u>. Nashville, TN: Thomas Nelson, 2003.

Nystrom, David P. The NIV Application Commentary: James. Grand Rapids, MI: Zondervan, 1997.

Peterson, Eugene H. As Kingfishers Catch Fire. Colorado Springs, CO: WaterBrook, 2018.

Poteat, Gordon. The Interpreter's Bible, Vol. 12 – James, George A. Buttrick, ed. New York: Abingdon, 1957.

Sabanda, Sibbs. Working in a Uniquely Christian Way. Las Vegas: Self-Published, 2022.

Sammis, John. Hymnal.net, https://www.hymnal.net/en/hymn/h/582, Accessed 7 Apr. 2023.

Sarna, Nahum M. Understanding Genesis. New York: Schocken Books, 1966.

Stamm, Raymond. The Interpreter's Bible. Ed. George A. Buttrick. Vol. 10. New York: Abingdon, 1953.

Tarrants, Thomas. "Pride and Humility." C.S. Lewis Institute, https://www.cslewisinstitute.org/resources/pride-and-humility/, Accessed 8 Aug 2022.

"The State of Missouri." Netstate.Com, 28 Jul. 2017, https://www.netstate.com/states/intro/mo_intro.htm. Accessed 6 Apr. 2023.

Wilkins, Michael J. The NIV Application Commentary: Matthew. Grand Rapids: Zondervan, 2004.

For author interviews or more information contact:

Mark T. Goodman
C/O Advantage Books
info@advbooks.com

To purchase additional copies of these books, visit our bookstore at
www.advbookstore.com

Orlando, Florida, USA
"we bring dreams to life"™
www.advbookstore.com

www.ingramcontent.com/pod-product-compliance
Lightning Source LLC
Chambersburg PA
CBHW051001060726
47593CB00018B/2074